FAITH LEGACIES

Guide for Faith-Based Nonprofits
To Reach Thousands and Raise Millions
"Planting Good Works and Producing Good Fruit"

"Planting Good Works to Produce Good Fruit"

By Dr. Margaret Jamal

Front and back cover photos by: Dr. A. Jamal of Spirit Led Media

Pro 25:2
Psa 50:14
Deu 8:18
Psa 18:49

This book was printed in the United States of America.

Dedication

This is dedicated to Almighty God,
His people and His works.

My family Rev. Dr. Aaron Jamal,
Gina, Asia, Joshua, Elijah, (Aisha)

In loving memory of my mother and mentor
Rev. Hazel (Mercer) Fort
And the Mercer's Faith Legacy
Archie, Sarah, Ruth, Margaret, Hazel, Howard

Thanks to
Rev. Edwin & First Lady Wilma Perry &
Fillmore Christian House of Prayer Community Church
Spirit Led Ministries
My other Siblings: Abdallah, Hazel Renae & Gina Ruth
My loving aunts, uncles, nieces, nephews and cousins
Friends and supporters
Midge Lansat and the
Healing and Creative Arts Center
Sheila White
G.O.A.L. International
for generous support

"Planting Good Works to Produce Good Fruit"

Table of Contents

Introduction

In his article entitled "Recession-Proof Nonprofit" Steven Malanga affirms that in recession, there is an increase in the demand for social services.

This is the season for the planters to mobilize their visions. It is a time when the world needs bold visionaries to settle down long enough to make good things happen.

Faith Legacies offers information, insight and strategies to help readers acquire the mindset, skills, relationships and resources needed in order to sustain an effective social service outreach. Faith Legacies includes a biblically based guide for planting good works to produce good fruit.

Faith Legacies is especially for people that have a "Do Something" attitude as opposed to turning away from today's problems. It includes a guide for finding and focusing on your calling, how to set up your program, find resources, and even how to write your grant proposals.

We are always most remembered for our works. It is time to start building the legacy that we want handed down for years to come. We need to plant legacies of love, hope, faith and good works.

Your instructions for this Faith Legacies book are simple.
1) Learn what it teaches. 2) Apply what you learn.
3) Practice what you understand. 4) And share what you did.

Chapter One Planting Good works

There are basically two types of people needed in order to start and continue good works. These are the *Planters* and the *Waterers*.

The planter gets things started, but finds it difficult to keep things going. Others rarely *catch their vision* because they simply do not have their way of thinking. Planters need to learn how to write the vision to make it plain so that others will run with it.

Now he that planteth and he that watereth are one: and every man shall receive his own reward according to his own labour. 9For we are labourers together with God: ye are God's husbandry, ye are God's building.
1 Cor 3:8 - 9 (KJV)

Planters have a difficult time getting others to truly follow them because by the time someone *almost* catches up, they have already moved on to the next phase. Meanwhile, their willing followers are still trying to find out where they fit.

 Planters are not necessarily the best at personal development for others. While they are definitely leaders, they are not the "people persons" that followers tend to require in order to continue offering their support.

Planters appear to be flighty because they seldom stay with something long enough to see it progress into tangible success. Others often see planters as hard working more than "smart" working, with little to show for all of their laboring. Still many recognize them as great visionaries who are blessed with innovations.

Planters seldom get the opportunity to reap the benefits of their efforts. This is because their efforts are vast and many who profit from their labors are *not* moved to hunt them down in order to show their appreciation. However, planters should know that God sees all and that they will reap rewards in due season.

Many people reflect on the problems that they see and dare to imagine what they could do to make a difference. For reasons that are perhaps as diverse as the personalities themselves, very few people actually make serious plans to *do* something.

On October 6, 2008, I attended the funeral of a woman who chose to *do something* about the pain and suffering that she witnessed. I sat in the second row and listened as one-by-one, people stood at the podium to share remarks about how she impacted their lives. The woman who was being honored was Rev. Hazel Fort- affectionately referred to as Mother Fort.

It was not the showing that I had expected having known firsthand about her constant efforts to do for others. I admit that I was disappointed that there was not the capacity crowd that I felt this woman of great works should have attracted. Still I was comforted and even honored as I listened to the testimonies of her legacy.

Among the commenter's included Illinois' Congressman Danny Davis who vowed to speak of Rev. Fort on the floor of congress for CNN to broadcast her of love for others. There was also the new Police Superintendant, Dana Starks who stated that her name should be in history books to promote how much Mother Fort made an impact in her community. He even emotionally referred to her as *"his"* mother. There was Alderman Ed Smith who could barely contain his sentimental display as he spoke of how Rev. Fort (who served as a precinct captain) was his official chaplain for the 51st Ward. Even Mayor Daley sent a formal message of appreciation and condolences.

And among the dignitaries, were a few passionate reflections by several others in the community whose lives were changed through Mother Fort's love and good works. What I noticed most was how many people spoke of the way that they "knew her." Mother Fort was someone that gave of herself as well as her resources while meeting the needs of others. The great impact that she left was apparent even in the small numbers that were present.

Paul wrote that " we are labourers together with God." Still it is not often that we are able to witness the fruit of our labor. It is encouraging to hear the testimonies of the good works planted in lives by one of God's laborers.

How many of us are able to say that those who speak of us will be able to reflect upon our good works? We all have works, but what makes them *good* is how they make a difference in the lives of others.

Paul also explains that there are planters and there are waters. I believe that the planters are those who began the legacies according to their faith. Their faith legacies are efforts that impact others to the degree that someone is moved to *continue* their works.

Mother Fort had founded a small community church in the heart of the west side. She had come from Mississippi with her sisters and raised her children on the west side of Chicago. But Mother Fort was actually following the lead of her older sister who had established her own faith legacy.

Their family name was *Mercer* and they would often refer to themselves as "The Mercers." Mother Fort's sister, Ruth (Mercer) Watson had founded another non-profit organization called the Lawndale Civics and Educational Club.

Mrs. Watson was moved by her convictions as a member of the African Methodist Episcopal (AME) church to do something to help the "colored" kids to have a better future than their parents. She often expressed feeling that education and culture held the keys to success, along with a religious upbringing. Mrs. Watson frequently invited people to attend Carey Tercentenary A.M.E. Church, located at 1448 South Homan Avenue, Chicago, Illinois. She wanted others to know about the rich heritage associated with her church organization to pass on to future generations. Mrs. Watson was certainly not hesitant about proclaiming the need for practicing one's faith.

Mrs. Watson was also an active member of the NAACP, The Northern District Association of Club Women and Girls and the ABC Youth Center in Lawndale and several other initiatives. Ironically, the same Congressman Davis also spoke at Mrs. Watson's funeral. However the Mayor giving tribute to Mrs. Watson was the late Richard J. Daley, the father of the Mayor who presented at Mother Fort's funeral.

Just as there was a legacy of political service with the Daley's, there was a history of good works being recognized in this family legacy. But the legacy was not in the *type* of community service as much as in *mindset* of *doing something* to make a difference. Even though Mrs. Watson passed on a legacy of doing good works to her sister, Mother Fort was not content to simply *water* the organization that her sister had planted.

Recognizing Your Season

Many people are recognizing a similar situation to Mrs. Watson and Mother Fort in *their* lives. As much as they would like to offer support for someone else, there is a nagging urge to launch another effort. They may be effective *waterers*, but are called to plant their own good works. They have a desire to labor in an area where they feel that they can make a difference.

There is a season for everything. There is a season and time that planting will be the primary purpose. For some, this is the time for getting things started. For others, it will be the time to keep things going.

When you feel that string urge to be the one to get things started, it may very well be your season to do so. If you are the type of person who is loyal and faithful, then it may be difficult to follow your own vision. It can be especially hard to move on while it remains apparent to you that the one that you are supporting is already struggling. However you may know in your heart that in your moving towards your destiny you will be even better positioned to offer greater support.

Knowing When it's Time to Move On

It may seem hard to know *when* or if *it* is time for you to move on and out to your call to get something started. The time will announce itself so apparently that you will not be able to ignore its presence. This will be the time that you feel you are being led to take action with what is growing in your spirit. You may even experience a sense of urgency that causes unrest.

You may even begin to display impatience with others who you believe are operating below *their* potential. Actually the one that you are disappointed in is you. But the unproductiveness in others is frustrating because you witness more reminders of your own inactivity.

When you reach the peak of being so dissatisfied with yourself that you feel that you *have* to do *anything* rather than keep still-then *stop*. Take some breaths and prepare to plant your good works with planning. If you do not follow a structure and plan, you will soon find yourself reaching that same peak of frustration.

Uncovering Your Calling

But you may be asking, "How do I know for sure what God has called me to do?" In fact, you might be called to do a number of good works, but feel confused because you don't know which one to address first. In this book you will learn about a method that the LORD has given to help you to focus on one specific area of your calling.

It is important to find focus because broad based activities can waste time and energies. Many of us are passionate about many things that pull on our desire for purpose. We are visionaries who see multiple problems that concern us along with a whole lot of different solutions. And we generally feel like *we* need to do all of them at the same time. But it is essential to concentrate efforts on first doing *one* thing well.

After you first establish this one thing that you are called to address, then the miraculous is released. I believe that God is poised to pour out the resources that you need in order to sustain you. I have literally had people seek me out to give me money, help and other resources to support me in my outreach ministry of helping others. And once you establish a firm foundation with that one problem that you are called to address then you can move on to another area.

One of my students decided to launch an outreach that would help to promote women in business so that their businesses would succeed. She realized that it hurt her so much to feel like a failure that she did not want anyone else to suffer with that same feeling.

But at first she was set on starting other things that were more glamorous and could have been more fun and uplifting. These projects did not deal with helping others to eliminate that feeling of failure. It was obvious to me that she did not have her passion behind the other business that she talked about starting.

I found that without the passion that comes with following your calling, it's just a matter of time when you find yourself quitting. It's not because you're a failure but because you're trying to succeed in the wrong area. Now think about these points that I am about to share with you to consider. Point #1: As followers of Christ we are told to pick up our cross and follow him. Point #2: There is some oppression or suffering planted in us that we have experienced. Point #3: This suffering that we experienced can be used for good.

We *are* called to *overcome* the suffering that we will face. Your calling might be associated with something so hurtful that you avoid even *thinking* about it. But God wants you to be healed. Ignoring it will not heal it. However, seeking ways to help others overcome that pain will help bring healing to *you*.

When You Think Your Pain
is Not Bad Enough

Please be careful not to belittle your pain and suffering simply because it does not appear to be as bad as someone else. In one of my workshops a young lady nervously shared that she did not feel that she had anything to offer because she was from a good family and had been sheltered. However sensing her passion for service, I was sure that she understood deep pain in a way that only comes with experience.

As we explored a little deeper, she revealed that she had considered suicide when she was younger. It was not because she had suffered a traumatic experience, but that she felt worthless and almost invisible. She even wished that something bad could happen so that she could have an excuse for how she felt. She was isolated and lonely.

Fortunately, I was able to show my student that the pain that she experienced is one that has caused great hardship for others. She finally realized that her struggle was just as significant as someone who experienced incarceration or some other tragedy. She came to understand that her perspective was valuable and greatly needed in order to help others who may also be tempted to end their lives for similar reasons.

"Planting Good Works to Produce Good Fruit"

Chapter Two **Accepting Your Role as Problem Solver**

- *Answering the Call to Eliminate Problems*
- *Focusing On Eliminating A Specific Problem*
- *Determining the Problems Exercise*
- *Focusing On a Specific Problem*

Answering the Call
to Eliminate Problems

So as we read along in Luke 4: 18, Jesus found the passage in the book and then read, "the Spirit of the Lord is upon Me Because He hath anointed Me to preach the gospel to the poor; He hath sent Me to heal the brokenhearted, to preach deliverance to the captives and recovering of sight to the blind; To set at liberty them that are bruised; To preach the acceptable year of the LORD."

In this statement Jesus revealed several problems that He was called to address. The problems included: poverty, brokenhearted-ness, blindness, captivity, and that term bruised also means battered, beaten and oppressed. The solutions to these problems included healing, preaching, recovery and deliverance. Now others might look at those same problems and come up with different solutions. But the solutions that Jesus applied were the ones that *He* was equipped to carry out.

Following Jesus' example, the problems that you will work to eliminate will be ones that God has anointed *you* to eliminate. You need to also know that the Spirit of the LORD must be upon you and that your commission comes with power. God gives you the power, favor and resources to carry out His will in your life.

Once you identify the problems that you are called to eliminate, you need to do as Jesus did and move forward in action- not looking back. You need to expect to be successful because this is not about you or your ability, but about God using you to bring solutions in the lives of others.

People have so many needs that if you try to meet all of them you will spend most of your time running around confused and drained. This is why we teach that you should first focus on the problem that you are *called* to *eliminate*. Every problem has its own set of needs for the clients that are being serviced; the staff that serves and assists; the partners that support and the donors that contribute. They all have needs.

However when you focus on a particular area or problem, then the response to needs are also more focused. The needs are related rather than scattered so that it is easier to plan strategies to meet those needs.

My experience taught me that even in trying to determine a problem to address; I needed to establish an understanding concerning what may be considered a problem. In human services I define a problem as something that causes pain, suffering or hardship. This gives me a reference to decide if something warrants the efforts of working towards a solution.

Therefore if I am presented with an issue that is said by someone to be a problem, I ask "how does this issue cause pain, suffering or hardship?" If I am not able to clearly express how this issue causes pain, suffering or hardship, then it will not be identified as a problem.

One of the challenges for many social entrepreneurs is that they are not committed to eliminating *one specific* problem. This can cause them to lose focus and stray from their purpose. This confusion will affect all of the support and resources. Each project must be planned according to the problem that is being eliminated.

The need for resources increases with every problem. Therefore if there are multiple problems that are being addressed at one time, the director has to find more money and resources in order to eliminate each one.

Generally people that have a personal stake and experience with a problem are more apt to stick with addressing it for a longer period of time. They find something that is fulfilling enough to do even without the need for outside appreciation. They would work to eliminate the problem without pay if needed. Their commitment will inspire them to learn how to become experts in their area. As experts, they are more likely to see significant progress in doing away with their problems.

Focusing on Eliminating
a Specific Problem

In order to be most effective it is important for you to have the goal to *eliminate* a specific problem. Trying to eliminate a problem may appear to be a huge task, but we have successes to model in those who sought to rid the world of specific areas of pain and suffering.

For example the program called Mothers Against Drunk Driving has a mission to completely eliminate drunk driving in the United States. According to a 2006 press release, the organizer and founding president of Mothers Against Drunk Driving also called (MADD) is Candy Lightner whose 13 year old daughter was killed by a drunk driver. Candy Lightner stated the following, "I promised myself on the day of Cari's death that I would fight to make this needless homicide count for something positive in the years ahead."

The pain and suffering that drunken driving caused Ms. Lightner was the death of her daughter. In eliminating drunken driving, she would also eliminate the suffering and destruction that vehicular homicide causes.

It takes little effort to deviate from the original purpose of an organization when there is more than one problem being addressed. However with the focus on a single problem, it is easier to recognize if that particular problem is being pushed aside for other interests.

In the example of MADD, Ms. Lightener was faced with an issue that challenged her own original mission to eliminate drunken driving. By 1985, many MADD leaders were calling for the criminalization of all driving after drinking any amount of alcoholic beverage. Ms. Lightner disagreed with this and stated that police ought to be concentrating their resources on arresting drunk drivers, not those drivers who happen to have been drinking.

Ms. Lightner stated that MADD "has become far more neo-prohibitionist than I had ever wanted or envisioned ... I didn't start MADD to deal with alcohol. I started MADD to deal with the issue of drunk driving".

It is up to the original visionary to keep the focus of a mission. When an organization expands, it attracts other people who may not agree with the original purpose. Other people who have suffered with problems similar to the visionary may reason that the mission should be altered.

When you are faced with having a number of problems that concern you, it helps to have a method of determining which problem you should address first. This does not mean that you cannot address other problems later. However you need a single focus to develop in order to have a foundation strong enough to sustain the challenges that will come from supporters and others.

Determining the Problems Exercise

The "Determining the Problems" exercise is developed to uncover heartfelt commitments in order to launch an effective solution driven project. This system helps participants to look at their concerns objectively to help focus upon which issue is most pressing to them. This most pressing issue will be the concern that causes someone to stick to their efforts even in the face of difficult challenges.

The *Determining the Problems* exercise included in this book requires you to name your problems with short titles. Participants are required to restrict their problem titles to between one and three words. The purpose for limiting the description to between one and three words is because the resources for addressing those problems will be found quicker with short descriptive keywords. When searching for resources and information that can help to develop or sustain a project, knowing certain key words will help to narrow the search results.

In order to decide upon the problems that you might be called to eliminate, consider your thoughtful responses to the following:
A) What suffering or pain have you experienced that you strongly desire to see eliminated? This could be something that you experienced as a child or in later years. This could be something that someone else caused but still resulted in your suffering.

For example if you suffered from alcoholism as an alcoholic, then you may list alcoholism as a problem. On the other hand if you were a child of an alcoholic parent the problem still relates to alcoholism, but you might list the problem as an "alcoholic parent."

Both situations could result in directly causing you pain and suffering. However, if you worked at a substance abuse clinic without ever having to experience direct personal addiction in some form, then alcoholism may not be an appropriate problem for you in this exercise.

Follow these simple steps to determine a list of problems that you may be called to help eliminate in the lives of others.

Step 1: Make a list of up to 5 problems that you have overcome. Keep in mind that a problem is something that causes pain suffering or hardship. We must first admit that we have in fact pressed through situations that caused pain, suffering and hardship. For example, substance abuse is a problem. Unemployment could also be a problem. It could clearly be explained how each of those problems cause pain, suffering and hardship. Remember that your problems should be 1 to 3 word descriptions.

In order to help organize your efforts a *Determining the Problem* Table is provided. The First column is for listing up to five personal experiences that you believe are problems. The other five columns are designed to help participants determine if they have listed the types of problems that they could commit to addressing for a significant period of time.

Step 2: Place your list of problems in the first column of the Determine the Problem table.

Step 3: Take the time to carefully consider the statements in the following columns. Place an "X" or check the spaces where the statement is true in regards to that particular problem. There is a blank table on A in the Appendices section, at the end of the book for you to use to determine your primary problem.

Step 4: Circle the problems in the form that have 5 checks or X's. You will use these results for the next step. NOTE: If none of your problems have 5 checks, you are probably not committed to finding your calling at this time.

NOTE: See how the table is completed in the example on the next page

Determine the Problem Table

Place an X in the box(es) next to the problem where the statement is true.

Problems (List the problems that you have experienced)	I strongly desire to eliminate this problem	This problem has caused me personal pain & suffering	I am personally responsible for doing something about this problem	It disturbs me to hear about someone else suffering from this problem	God has called me to help eliminate this problem	TOTALS
1. unemployment	X	X	X	X		4
2. inadequate healthcare	X			X		2
3. drunk driving	X	X	X	X	X	5
4. juvenile incarceration	X	X	X	X	X	5
5. lack of education	X	X				2

Focusing On a Specific Problem

In order to narrow the focus (from the list developed from the Primary problem exercise), you will rate each problem against each other.

Step 1: Using your list from the previous step, write up to 5 problems in the boxes provided in the top of the form of the Focus on the problem sheet.

Step 2: For each row, compare the problems where the boxes are not shaded. Imagine two people in front of you suffering from the problems being considered. Then decide which one of the problems you would be most compelled to address first. Mark the circle that represents the problem that you would address first.

Step 3: After comparing each problem (one row at a time) the circles under the problems are either marked with an "X" or empty. Count the total number of marks one column at a time, placing that total in the boxes provided below.

The total number of marks indicates the priority of importance when each problem is assessed objectively. See the table illustration.

There is a blank form on B in the Appendices section at the end of the book for you to use to focus on your primary problem.

Once all of the problems have been compared and rated in order of priority, it becomes easier to organize targeted plans, strategies and resources.

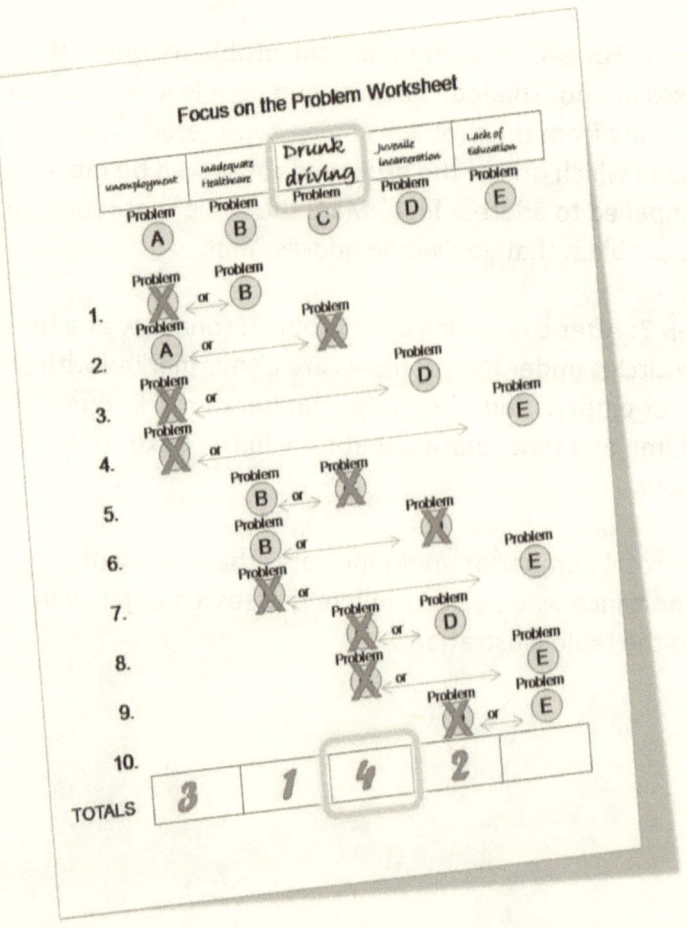

"Planting Good Works to Produce Good Fruit"

Chapter Three Identifying a Target Population

- *Identify Tangible Beneficiaries*
- *The Purpose for Selecting a Target Population*
- *The Who's Your Client Exercise*

Identify Tangible Beneficiaries

Any effort to eliminate a problem needs to identify tangible beneficiaries of its success. Tangible beneficiaries are those whose lives are clearly *improved* as a result of their participation. Without establishing a profile of tangible beneficiaries, it is difficult to demonstrate *how*, and *to what extent* a program is working.

For example, if you plan to launch a program to eliminate smoking cigarettes, you may include special nutrition workshops. These workshops could be so effective that non-smokers sign up to attend. However a post assessment would produce negative responses when non-smokers are asked if this workshop helped them in their ability to stop smoking. Any reference made to smoking would be irrelevant to them. They would also find that they would not have much in common with the smokers who are attending the sessions.

The resource materials would not be useful to non-smokers because those materials would be intended to support the efforts of the organization to eliminate smoking. When evaluating the effectiveness of the workshops, non-smokers would not state that these workshops helped them to stop smoking.

On the other hand, the target population of smokers would better understand the connection of the nutritional workshops as they relate to eliminating smoking. They would also be able to relate to those evaluation questions that reference how the workshops have helped them to eliminate smoking.

The Purpose for Selecting a Target Population

Selecting a target population is important, because it helps to build the tools for measuring success. It also helps to focus the program development. If a visionary has a vision to eliminate smoking, then the intervention should be targeted to serve people who smoke. If the problem is underage smoking, then this helps to be even more specific in establishing a target population.

The more general the target population, the more work will be required to accommodate the broad based needs. A program that is focused upon eliminating smoking with adolescents must address a number of concerns that would not be needed for adult intervention efforts. For example, youth focused social services are required to have appropriate background checks for those adults that will be working with young participants.

The intervention services for youth may also need to consider their short attention span. There may also be a need to get parental permission for certain activities. These are just some of the considerations that may arise based upon the target population that is established.

Establishing a target population needs to be done with great thought and consideration. In some situations, the target population is established with the vision. An example of this is the Young Women's Christian Association, commonly referred to as the YWCA. Their mission statement demonstrates an example that supports the previous lesson for focusing on eliminating a specific problem.

According to their mission statement, the problem that the YWCA is committed to eliminate is racism. They also indicate a target population of young women that they clearly plan to support. With the target population so well defined, it is easy for the YWCA to plan intervention activities and evaluation plans. It is also easier to research potential donors who want to help their target population.

Your target population is also referred to as your consumers or clients. The client is anyone who makes use of your services. As you continue to build your organization, it will be to your advantage to understand and adapt a very important phrase that we pass on to all of our students. That phrase is, "Everybody is not my client." There may be a lot of people who fit your profile according to your target population. However until they agree that they need you and agree to use your services to eliminate their problem, they are *not your clients*.

Consider the following scenario: A middle aged man enters the door of a recovery support program especially developed for people who have been incarcerated and have substance abuse issues. This man informs a receptionist at the front desk that he has never been arrested, but smokes a little marijuana. He states that the reason that he has come to this organization is because he needs a job. He had heard that this program helped ex-offenders to get jobs. Upon further inquiry the receptionist learns that this man has a resume and work experience that could help him easily qualify for a position that was recently posted.

While this program has an objective to help people to get jobs, they have a mandate and responsibility to find jobs for certain types of people. They are being funded to find employment specifically for former prison inmates who have had substance abuse issues.

It might be easier for the organization to place this man in employment, because he is not hindered by the stigma of being an ex-offender. However if this man fills the position, then there would be one less opportunity to have it filled by a true client for this program.

The dilemma described in the passage above is played out in many organizations. The staff is often faced with their desire to help, along with their obligation to work within certain guidelines. A dedicated employee may seek to be a problem solver for clients, but have trouble distinguishing a qualified client from a potential client.

A qualified client is one that has been assessed and found to fit the required profile for receiving services. A qualified client has the required problems, needs and background that the program is designed to accommodate.

Many organizations have difficulty with indoctrinating their staff and support regarding the treatment of only qualified clients. Likewise many workers are simply not certain about when or if they are able to go beyond the given criteria for participation. For this reason, organizational leaders will do well to establish clear and readily understood guidelines for identifying a client.

The Who's Your Client Exercise

The next exercise includes a worksheet called "Who's Your Client?" The *Who's Your Client?* worksheet is developed to help people to establish their target populations. This will help determine who will benefit from your being successful with eliminating the problem. You will narrow the focus to describe the type of people that you are committed to serve.

You should also keep in mind that once your program is ready, your potential clients have to be drawn to the services that you are offering. This process of drawing people to your services requires marketing. Effective marketing efforts may be very difficult to plan without an established target population.

A challenge that I found for settling upon a target population included being concerned about missing opportunities because of such a narrow focus. Many people have difficulty settling upon a target population because they do not want to leave any one out. However those who specialize and target people who they can best relate to, will have a better chance with being successful. Think about it. If you were going to seek service from someone, would you rather be helped by someone that can truly relate to your problem? Or would you be fine with a one size fits all approach? Would you feel slighted by a service provider who insists upon solutions that they only read about? Would you not feel insulted with someone using terms such as "you are supposed to know..." or "you are supposed to be..." based upon practices that they learned just to satisfy their license or certification requirements?

However if you have personally been subjected to the experiences or problems that you are working to eliminate, then you have a better chance of relating to your client. The type of people that you can personally relate to should be among your primary target population.

If someone wants to serve substance abusers without having been victimized by substance addiction, that person's solutions to the problem of substance abuse may not be practical. The complexities of human services are magnified when being addressed by those who cannot relate. Our responses to expressed needs are generally not empathetic to struggles that we have not experienced for ourselves.

In the example of having a problem with substance abuse, it is possible that a service provider was victimized by having a parent, child or care giver that struggled with drug addiction. This connection will at least give this person a way to relate from a realistic point of view. Service providers may offer better services for a longer time when they can relate to those that they serve. With this in mind consider beginning with a target population of people most like yourself in their struggles. This is why the "Who's Your Client?" exercise is so crucial. The "Determine the Problem" lesson helps to identify the service that addresses a personal area of pain and suffering.

The "Who's Your Client?" worksheet will connect the results of the earlier lesson by developing a profile of the clients who will benefit from eliminating the pain and suffering.

This process will answer the questions such as:
1) Who benefits from this problem being eliminated?
2) How would you describe your target population?

Use the sample *Who's Your Client Worksheet* as a model for detailing the type of information that will help identify your target population. You do not have to consider all of the categories given. In addition, you may add categories according to what you know about your area of interest.

This exercise may give you a greater appreciation for why you should be an expert in a specific area. If you had not experienced suffering in an area, it would be difficult to understand how to profile the type of people that you should be servicing.

Who's Your Client Worksheet
Client Profile Summary

Primary Problem that I am committed to eliminating is:_____

The Client profile of my target population includes the following:_____

Personal Characteristics (age range, gender, ethnic background, etc.)

_____

Social Challenges (ex-offender, unemployed, etc.)

_____

_____

Other Concerns (obesity, Mental Health, veteran, etc.)

_____

_____

Geographic location

City:_____	State:_____
Zip/Postal Code:_____	County:_____
Ward:_____	Precinct:_____
Congressional District:_____	Senatorial District:_____
Region:_____	Country:_____
Population:_____	Unemployment Rate:_____
Poverty Rate:_____	Crime Rate:_____
Other stats (explain):_____	

"Planting Good Works to Produce Good Fruit"

Chapter Four **Assessing Needs**

- *Purpose for Needs Assessments*
- *Planning a Needs Assessment,*
- *Understanding Partner Needs*
- *Identifying Organizational Needs*
- *Recognizing That Donors Have Needs*

After uncovering the profile for your target population of clients, it is time to answer the question, "What does my client need in order to stop suffering from the problem that I am committed to eliminating?" This is not an easy question to answer. But it is even more difficult to answer for anyone who has not suffered from the problem at all. This is why the "What's the Problem?" exercise is so important to work through honestly. Also, the "Who's Your Client?" exercise was important to help plan focused and targeted services that will provide a favorable response to client needs.

The people that have suffered from the problem that you are committed to eliminating have a need for services that will lead to overcoming that problem. Your client needs to feel a sense of relief from the pain and suffering caused by that problem.

There are two primary issues that must be considered in order to provide successful solutions to societal problems. The first issue is whether or not solving the particular problem will *eliminate* the pain and suffering that has been identified. The second issue is whether or not the target population *agrees* that the problem stated is the problem that *they* want to eliminate. This second issue is one of the reasons that preparing a good *needs assessment* is critical.

After you have settled upon a problem to eliminate and have also developed a client profile of your target population, it's time to plan your response to your client needs. The needs that concern you should be restricted to those needs that result from having the problem that you are committed to eliminating. For example, if your client needs housing, but the lack of housing does not influence the problem that you are eliminating, then the need for housing will not be your concern. However if the lack of housing hinders your ability to service your client, then this need should be factored into your options for possible solutions to your client's problem.

Whatever response you plan to give should be in consideration of what your target population or client needs in order to get relief from his or her problem.

In some cases you may be compelled to advocate on behalf of your client because the standard treatments simply do not work. This may especially be a concern for those receiving government funds or grants from rigid donors. You may have to be innovative in how you meet the needs of your clients while still meeting the requirements of the donor.

For example a person with the problem of substance abuse that has gainful employment may not be in need of vocational training. It could be a waste your client's valuable time to force him or her to participate in vocational training simply because it is a requirement for your program. However there may be a module in your vocational training that includes a personality assessment.

If your client expressed a need to have better communication and acceptance in the workplace, the personality assessment tool could be used. In this case the specific section that addresses the personality assessment should be what is made available to your client without forcing the entire vocational training service.

Your solution to the problem should be designed to address the specific needs that arise from that problem. For example, imagine that you have a client who suffers from drug addiction that is also a homeless veteran, with other health problems. In this example, the problem that you are committed to eliminate is *only* substance abuse. However, a homeless client is difficult to keep engaged with services due to challenges associated with unstable housing.

The stress of not having stabile housing may hinder the treatment services from lasting, because your client is self medicating the stressful feelings with drugs. The health issues may also contribute to doctors prescribing medications that trigger the desire for narcotics.

I am aware of an example of a doctor that prescribed the drug Vicodin for a client that had been in a drug recovery program. This client had remained free from heroin use for over 4 years. The feelings that occurred with the Vicodin drug triggered a desire to maintain the euphorically numbing feeling that heroin once provided. After the Vicodin bottle was emptied this person went back into the streets in search of heroin.

When an organization designs solutions that are specific to the particular problems of a client, there is a greater likelihood that the client will willingly and successfully engage in the program activities.

Purpose for Needs Assessments

A needs assessment will help to determine the nature and severity of the problem that is being eliminated for your clients. Without knowing the nature and impact of the problem, it is impossible to decide how to eliminate it. Data from the needs assessment can also help to gain support and resources for prevention and intervention projects.

A baseline needs assessment provides knowledge of client related conditions *before* engaging in a project or program.   This type of assessment is a necessary first step in conducting an evaluation of a program's effectiveness. When a baseline assessment is given to a client before introducing a new activity, it is easier to monitor and record the extent that a problem has declined.

Our small congregation was comprised of a dedicated and gifted group who had hearts to serve. We had an outreach ministry that shared music and resources with the community as well as with other churches. We were pretty much a mission extension of the church in Chicago that launched our ministry.

One day during a bible study we asked the membership what they thought that we could do to reach more people. Someone stated that we needed to meet the needs of the poor people in the community. The needs were great in our community because of the high poverty level.

In developing our assessment, we included a checklist for respondents to indicate what they considered to be their greatest needs. We also asked about what they already were able to access. Many of those who were in the extreme poverty level did not indicate a high need for food. They were more interested in funds to pay bills.

At the time, our primary outreach services included an after school tutoring program and a food distribution service for low income recipients. But we realized that we could still do something to help by offering free food. We realized that if we offered a family $250 dollars worth of free food each month, that family could use their savings to pay other bills such as utility, transportation, etc.

Our evaluation would need to include a question about being able to cover more bills due to the increased access to food. Without the baseline assessment, we would not have known how people really felt about their needs. We would not have known how to word our evaluation to actually reflect how our services benefited our target population.

A Pastor shared a situation in one of our workshops. The group later made comments about how it related to addressing the needs of the client. The Pastor shared how for many years he had a headache that would cause him extreme discomfort.

In his words, "Every time my headache came back I would go get my usual pain medicine. One day I decided to give in to my wife's insistence that I go to the doctor. The doctor said something to me that changed the way I viewed that headache for the rest of my life. He said that a headache is not normal and that it means that something is wrong. People are not supposed to have headaches like that on a regular basis. Up until then, I even referred to the pain in my head as 'my headache.'"

The Pastor also shared how the doctor explained that because he was simply taking pills to get rid of the pain, it made him think that the pills were actually making him better. This Pastor was only getting rid of the symptoms, which had been there to let him know that he had a serious problem.

A growing number of social entrepreneurs are coming to terms with the reality that *treating symptoms* rather than addressing underlying causes has resulted in a tremendous waste of resources. They are being encouraged to maximize resources by targeting efforts where they will make the greatest impact. They are also aware that the problem is not always obvious.

Planning a Needs Assessment

When planning a needs assessment, it should first be clear how the assessment will be used. For example, if a needs assessment will be used to develop the program activities then there may be more open ended questions. Open ended questions are questions that allow the respondent to give an answer that was not included in the document. An example of an opened question is, *"What services have you requested that you did not receive?"*

However, if the needs assessment is mainly to measure the client's perspective of *how much* a service is needed, the questions may include rating numbers. The following is an example of a rating question:

The service that you received was delivered in a timely fashion.

☐4 Strongly Agree	☐ 3Agree	☐ 2Disagree	☐ 1Strongly Disagree

The results of a needs assessment will help to design the type of intervention and or prevention activities and resources for developing a program

Examine the *Needs Assessment Planning Form* on the following page to see how to list hardships that are caused by, or result from the problem that you are committed to eliminate. This list will be used to allow potential clients to influence the type of services that will be offered to them.

The *Needs Assessment Planning Form* illustration demonstrates planning the needs for people suffering with substance abuse. Notice that the first related problem is homelessness. This issue has its own set of needs to address.

Needs Assessment Planning Form

Example

Primary problem of _____ *substance abuse* _____

The problem that I plan to eliminate causes my client to suffer with_____ *homelessness* _____
Therefore (he/ she) has a need for
1) _____ *housing assistance* _____
2) _____ *transitional housing options* _____
3) _____ *housing vouchers to cover rent* _____

Primary problem of _____

The problem that I plan to eliminate causes my client to suffer with_____
therefore (he/ she) has a need for
1) _____
2) _____
3) _____

The problem that I plan to eliminate causes my client to suffer with_____
therefore (he/ she) has a need for
1) _____
2) _____
3) _____

Understanding Partner Needs

If the leadership of an organization desires maximum input from the staff, they should elevate them to partners. A partner takes ownership while a staff worker takes a job. In order to get real contributions from the "partners" there are needs that they have which should be considered.

Partners need to:
• feel like their input to eliminate a problem matters.
• know that they will be in the loop with the flow of information.
• feel that they will be included with making decisions that affect them.
• know that they will be encouraged to take action and chances
• know that they will be supported even through the mistakes.

The list above for partners alternates between knowing and feeling certain ideas. This is because although something may be stated and even written as policy, if partners are not confident in the commitment from leadership, they will not trust in what is written or stated.

Newly formed grass roots organizations are often started by wonderful visionaries who are passionate about meeting the needs that they have observed and felt. These visionaries soon find that they want to address a growing number of related problems in many different ways. For example one such visionary (we will call her

Mother Snow) wanted to provide a "safe haven" for the children of parents that have been incarcerated and are often wandering the streets searching for love and attention.

One day a young girl in Mother Snow's Safe Haven asked Mother Snow about how to pronounce a word in her reading book. Mother Snow sat down to help the child struggle through her reading assignment. Mother Snow soon realized that many of her children were not doing well in school and needed help with basic reading and writing skills.

While trying to provide tutoring for these children, Mother Snow also found that these children were not eating properly and needed nutritional meals in order to function. After beginning a feeding program, Mother Snow was informed by some of the children that other people in the community and even people living with them were taking their the snacks from them.

Upon further inquiries, Mother Snow uncovered that many of her children were living in houses that were overrun with illegal and immoral activities. She also learned that (in some cases) visitors and family members were taking advantage of some of these children and abusing them.

Mother Snow tried to address every new problem that would arise until she finally found these needs to be overwhelming. Her own health began to suffer under the increasing stress of trying to protect and care for the children alone. Soon, Mother Snow's Safe Haven was closed to all of the children who were once comforted and sheltered from the streets. Mother Snow was broken hearted knowing that there was no one else who would take up the cause with the love and passion that she had.

Mother Snow once shared how when she was a young single mother, she had to work to support her children. This caused them to be alone with nothing constructive to do. Some of her children found themselves in tragic situations that she attributed to a lack of supervision.

Mother Snow did not know what she could have done differently, but felt that if her daughter could have just had a caring responsible home to stay in until she returned from work, things would have been different. She wanted to be for other parents what she wished someone would have been for her.

While Mother Snow was not the child in the streets, she suffered because of her own children being alone and unsupervised. Mother Snow was not trying to start a daycare or anything complicated. She just knew that there were predators looking for unsupervised children to corrupt. She knew that some of her own children had fallen victim to that element and felt the need to turn her pain into a passion for helping others.

Mother Snow felt that she let the children down because she was no longer able to supply the needs for the children. However, her original vision was simply to provide a "safe haven" that would allow these children to get off the streets. Mother Snow could have stayed with her original vision and then sought help from others who already had visions of providing tutoring, nutritional meals and child advocacy. It is important to understand that the original vision can become greatly compromised if other perceived needs begin to use up valuable resources.

In Mother Snow's case (and many others like her), her most valuable resource, which was the human resource, was over taxed to the point of burn out. When there is no clear plan for providing services, the problem that appears most urgent at the time is the one that gains the attention of a caring service provider. However the reactionary approach to service provision keeps organizations in crisis mode. This ever growing emergency status does not allow for the reflection, evaluation and capacity building that is needed to sustain an organization.

In order to develop an effective plan and process for meeting needs, the plan must begin with first identifying a single area of concern. The plan will be to eliminate the problem in those who are suffering rather than simply reducing the effects of a problem. The goal of eliminating a problem will help to target efforts towards the root causes of a problem.

For example, Mother Snow needed to stay committed to the problem of children being in the streets in harm's way. Then she could focus on her own ability to keep the youth out of the streets by giving them access to her facility. Her other efforts might be to find ways to keep them properly supervised. Once she enlisted help, she could feel satisfied that her goal to eliminate the children's unsafe exposure to the streets was being met. She could feel confident that she provided a safe haven for a given number of children.

Although her own children had received this type of support, Mother Snow was comforted in knowing that she was offering protection for others. She began to heal in her helping. She was not even concerned with whether the parents appreciated what she was doing. She knew that this was what was needed and she felt good helping other parents the way she had wished for help when she was a young mother.

Once she had established her reputation in this single area of need, she could attract additional support from other resources. Then the other problems that would arise could be addressed by those who specialize in those areas. These specialists could become partners committed to the same end result- meeting the needs of the clients to eliminate their problems.

When recruiting partners to form collaborative efforts, remember that they also have fundamental needs in order to maintain a working partnership. Your efforts to give a favorable response to those needs can greatly enhance your capability to deliver relevant services without experiencing burn out. The word collaboration contains the words "co" and "labor" indicating that there will be entities *laboring together*. You and your collaborators will labor or work together towards common results.

The ability to collaborate effectively will allow projects to work better because it relieves the burden of trying to meet all of the needs alone. People can plan and respond much better when they feel that they have the help and resources that they need. Collaboration offers a sense of empowerment through shared responsibility.

Identifying Organizational Needs

Organizational needs include: adequate facility, adequate staffing, effective leadership, opportunity for growth and expansion along with appropriate financial support. The leadership of an organization is crucial and will determine the organization's ability to sustain and even expand.

The Board of Directors provides the oversight of an organization. This board will offer direction to the primary leadership. The board members also provide support and encouragement for the one who is responsible for managing the organization. The primary makeup of a Board of Directors includes a Chair, Secretary and Treasurer. Each board member is responsible for making sure that the organization stays focused on achieving the stated goals. Board members also assume legal responsibility and liability for the conduct of an organization.

A good Board is able to respond to the funding needs of an organization through individual contributions as well as referrals and fund raising initiatives. Each board member must take on the responsibility of assuring that the organization remains solvent and productive. Board members are concerned with the fiscal as well as the program management of the organization.

Board members may also be divided into committees that concentrate on specific areas. These areas may include: a budget committee which oversees and approves the organizational and project budgets; an executive committee which addresses policies and legal agreements; a finance committee which is dedicated to making decisions about investments and fund raising activities; a public relations committee which is responsible for promoting and maintaining a good and inviting public image for the organization. A member of the board is selected to head each committee although each committee participant may not be an actual board member.

Board members should be selected according to how they will help meet the overall goals and objectives of an organization according to the stated mission. With this in mind, board members should have a vested interest in the carrying out the mission, goals and objectives of the organization. Therefore the makeup of board members should reflect the interest of the population that will be serviced according the organization's stated mission, goals and objectives.

For example, an organization with a mission to service at-risk youth should include board members that have experience or a genuine interest with at-risk youth. The board membership should also include someone who has been an at-risk youth to gain a realistic perspective of the needs that should be addressed.

Since the board members are expected to address the fiscal management the board should include someone who is knowledgeable about finances and fund raising. A well rounded board should include members that are proficient in addressing each aspect of the mission statement, goals and objectives that are expressed by the organization.

The ideal board of directors will also be able to address the organization's legal, financial, technical and resource concerns as well as provide moral support and encouragement for success.

Here is a sample request developed by Rev. Edwin Perry for his non-profit that summarizes what an organization might submit to a potential board member.

As a potential Board member of Christians Building Urban Communities, we ask that you consider the following minimum expectations:
-Will bring knowledge and influence to help to move this organization to another level
-Help to oversee policies & procedures
-Help to raise funds
-Bring forth volunteers and other resources
-Help us to complete our projects
-Assist with fiscal oversight
-Help with the overall governance of the organization
-Serve as legal representative for contract approvals

Recognizing That Donors Have Needs

Donors have so many different reasons for giving. A representative from a money management firm once told me that in his years of experience he saw two great motivators for the wealthy to give. He said one is fear and the other is greed. I somewhat understood the fear, but needed more clarity with how greed could prompt a wealthy person to give. He explained that if donors can see how their giving can increase their own wealth in tax deductions or favors (directly or indirectly) they can be convinced to make considerable donations.

I was relieved to meet someone who formed an organization that would encourage yet another reason to give, which is genuine love and caring for the welfare of others.

J.T. "Dock" Houk's writings reflect someone on a mission to change the thinking of those wealthy individuals who have the ability to alleviate human suffering, but for some reason choose not to contribute. He also passionately promotes empowering those who may feel insignificant to realize that everyone can have a place in making the world better.

It has sometimes been difficult to research and uncover the vast wealth that exists while also researching the fixable suffering that also exists. There are so many hurting children who are looking to us and saying "fix it." Yet there are many enabled individuals and organizations in our world that have seemingly turned their heads away from the problems. Some have expressed that they did not see how their contribution could make a difference.

Dock Houk once made a statement in a seminar that we sponsored which had a profound effect on me. He stated that he felt that we needed to "find ways to minister to the donor." That is when I realized that donors also have needs.

Donors need to feel confident that they are investing in an organization that will prove their ability to improve the lives of those who suffer from the problem being eliminated. They also need to:
• know that their donations are being given to good stewards.
• feel like their donations are investments that have a lasting positive impact on eliminating a problem.
• feel like their contributions (however small) will be appreciated.
• feel like an organization is not solely dependent upon them to sustain their efforts.

But most of all, I believe that donors need our prayers and encouragement. They need to be viewed as much more than a paycheck. Donors are also partners who have a stake in the success of whatever initiative that they support.

My book called "National Treasures – U.S. Foundations Grants" includes a list of donors who are clearly committed to giving to causes that will make the world better for underprivileged people.   In my research, I especially selected those donors that had a history of giving to faith-based causes.

It occurred to me that the donors featured in the National Treasures book are in need of significant prayer covering.

After you get the National Treasures-U.S. Foundation Grants book, begin praying for your intended donors immediately. Also pray that you will have favor with them.

You may even send them a letter of appreciation before you send one asking for money. Let them know that you appreciate their concern making the world better through their generosity.

Even if you are turned down at first, continue praying for them and encouraging them. You will be surprised to see how this simple gesture of support can transform a rejection letter into a cheerful gift.

"Planting Good Works to Produce Good Fruit"

Chapter Five R.A.T.E.S.™ Development

- *The Birth of R.A.T.E.S.™*
- *The Faith Connection to Social Services*
- *Making the Decision and Commitment*

The Birth of R.A.T.E.S.™

The Faith Legacy that began with Mother Fort, who was introduced in the first chapter, blossomed into many good works. Her son continued as the Pastor of the church that she planted. He is joined by his wife who oversees the food pantry along with nieces, nephews, church members and friends who help serve the community each week.

My portion of Mother Fort's vision as the eldest daughter was to embrace the task of encouraging and assisting ministry leadership to unite in order to better serve their communities. My target population (like Mother Fort's) remains the hurt, abused and neglected youth. To this end, I sought to learn strategies for attracting f funds and resources. I was even sent to Washington D.C. to learn the intricacies of the grant award process.

I found that even though I understood the mechanics of grant proposal writing, I felt distressed with getting funds to do a project that I really did not want to do. At the same time I felt that people who really wanted to work in a particular area should know how to get the funds and resources needed to be successful. I wanted to develop a program to get financial support for what I felt led to do rather than just do something because money was being offered for it.

I also realized that organizations that tried to stay afloat on their own had a difficult time. But those that were connected with other productive organizations helped each other to sustain. I concluded that in order to launch and sustain a results driven organization, we needed to partner with others. We needed to have other contributors who would know how to tap into their own resources for the good of overall success. We also needed to know how to work together to serve common clients while realizing that each organization is needed in order to see success. In other words, we needed to enhance our ability to succeed by working together.

However, most of the organizations did not know how to work with others. Many were not certain about what they offered or what they needed. They still required help with defining themselves so that they could assess and utilize their own resources.

We did not have a "user friendly" instrument that could help us to understand ourselves. We also lacked the ability to communicate our needs and assets in order to service our mutual clients.

We formed a non-profit initiative dedicated to empowering others with knowledge and skills to establish sustainable social service programs. I called this the R.A.T.E.S.™ Foundation. As the director of the R.A.T.E.S.™ Foundation I was compelled by a commission and an anointing to instruct others about the R.A.T.E.S.™ principles for organizational development. These principles are included in the name. The "R" is for Responsibility, "A" for Accountability, "T" for Technical ability, "E" for Evaluation ability and "S" for Sustain ability.

R.A.T.E.S.™ Development proved to be a valuable tool for first getting participants to have a universally understood platform for a standard of planning, assessment and operation. We could be confident that those organizations that understand and operate according to the R.A.T.E.S.™ principles would at least have a foundation that we could all build upon. We could also communicate our practices according to the language of R.A.T.E.S.™ to help determine where each participating organization would fit into each other's efforts.

Each R.A.T.E.S.™ principle is biblically based and is described as follows:
Response-ability is having and demonstrating the ability to give a favorable response to problems and needs. This includes the needs of the client, staff, partners, donors and the organization as a whole. Learning Goal: Learn to develop the fundamental elements for problem and basic needs statements. Participants will first learn a technique to focus upon a specific problem to eliminate. This process is designed to encourage and demonstrate commitment to make a measurable improvement in society. Then problem and needs statements will be developed with projected solutions for meeting those needs.

Jesus responded to tangible needs in addition to preaching the Gospel. He fed five thousand people. When his disciples pointed out that the people should go get something to eat, Jesus responded with "You give them what they need." Jesus trained the disciples and provided specific instructions. He then later empowered them to continue to carry out His works.

Account-ability is having and demonstrating the ability to account for program and fiscal activities along with associated resources. Learning Goal: Learn to develop a basic intake and attendance form to account for a client's qualification to participate in a program and to prove the level of participation. This information will also cover the development of budget summary and elements of a budget narrative to explain expenses.

Jesus accounted for the materials that He used. When He fed the five thousand, He accounted for the resources that He had. He asked the disciples about how many fishes and loaves they had available to use. Afterwards the scriptures documents how many basketfuls of scraps were left. Jesus even paid the temple tax. He gave us many examples of specific accountability with measurable results.

Jesus called individuals (Apostles) who were unique in what they brought to the group. Although He went to the masses, He made specific invitations to individuals to follow him. While Jesus allowed a broader audience to learn from him He did not permit everyone to follow him.

He had a set number of 12 that would be in his core relationship. Jesus called and mentored 12 and then sent out 72. He also had a specific number of two that were dispatched in an outreach effort. Each team of two was given specific procedures to follow while in the field.

I believe that most of today's churches are launched in ways contrary to making disciples. The mindset is to generate members in as many numbers as possible. However Jesus provided a model of mentoring a small foundation before branching out to reach the masses. Following this model would make churches more accountable overall.

Technical-ability is having and demonstrating the ability to apply technology in order to maximize productivity. It also includes having the ability to engage the technical communication, practices and policies that govern an area of interest. NOTE: More donors are requiring that grant seekers apply for grants exclusively online. Therefore those who are internet smart will have a better chance of beating out the competition. Also if you do not have a presence and email, you do not officially exist. Learning Goal: Learn how to assess and plan technological support according to needs as well as learn about the technical aspects involving the chosen area of interest. Additionally, this information addresses basic internet communications and tips for developing a basic client and resource support database along with a selling web presence and email access.

Jesus read the Scriptures in the synagogue, cast out demons, healed the sick and raised the dead. He also used scribes to document His works. He included studies concerning the policies and procedures in his area of interest. He was able to operate within the Jewish tradition because He studied it. He knew the gaps in services because He understood the context of the services and the rules that governed them. Jesus observed the technicalities concerning His area of interest in the Jewish culture which made Him irrefutable when He challenged the reigning authorities.

Evaluation-ability is having and demonstrating the ability to engage an independent and unbiased evaluator who will assess the strengths and challenges of your organization and related projects. The results of the evaluations will help develop strategies for ongoing improvements. The techniques for planning an evaluation will also help strengthen program structure and efficiency. Learning Goal: Learn how to plan an evaluation strategy to demonstrate project and organizational outcomes. Learn the basic elements for developing a logic model to demonstrate method and flow of evaluation.

Each project or program needs to be evaluated with methods that will provide objective assessments. The results of these assessments can help to determine the strengths and weaknesses of a project or even the overall program. An organization needs to think in terms of what systems are in place to assess organizational efficiency.

There is an excellent report commissioned by the W.K. Kellog Foundation on the results of a 2002 grantmaker's conference. The conference by Grantmakers for Effective Organizations, was in partnership with Forum of Regional Associations of Grantmakers, Grantmakers Evaluation Network. The report includes a section titled, "Measure for Measure: Evaluating Grantmaker Effectiveness. It describes how grantmakers should view their grantees with regards to the evaluation process. In the article the author begins with the following statement, "Grantmakers across the country regularly challenge their grantees to think in new ways about their own effectiveness and how to measure it."

Organizations may be apprehensive about evaluators because they represent a determining factor in regards to the type of funding as well as the amount that may be invested. For example, an evaluator may determine that an organization simply does not have the capacity to carry out the program for which it is requesting funds. This assessment is generally based upon answers to questions and observations. Some organizations have expressed concern in the questions that are being presented not being appropriate to assess how organizations are doing what they do.

Evaluations are typically based upon a pool of past experiences. Therefore if a "well run" youth program typically employs a project manager, secretary and bookkeeper and a certified youth social worker then other programs that lack in any of these areas may be considered to be running over capacity. I remember applying for a grant and stating that we would produce a multi-media video program in two weeks and receiving low points because the reader thought that it was not nearly enough time to complete such a project.

Likewise an evaluator may prepare questions about how something will take place with a preconception about how it could happen. We were once asked to list everything that our organization does by a program evaluator. The evaluator was immediately convinced that we do too much because of the list and because of our own limited paid staff. We were never asked who was responsible for each of the projects. The answers to that question would have shed some light on things.

For example, for the feeding program, we had women who volunteered to prepare the meals. To give out packaged food, we had people in the neighborhood that would pack the goods and help with distribution.

We began taking our youth in our youth program to other organizations that had services that we did not offer while helping them with skills that they did not have. An independent evaluation uncovered that our true expertise was in the ability to enlist services and support from and for other grass roots organizations. We were fortunate to have a funder that invited us to partner in the evaluation process.

The disciples of Jesus reported, "Even the demons submit to us in your name." They demonstrated that they had something to show for the power that they were given. They offered proof of change that occurred because of how Jesus influenced them. Also Jesus was able to report to the Father, the results of his mission on earth. Jesus said "I have not lost any that you have given me." He even had specific and measurable results.

Jesus initially recruited 12 and later sent out 72, demonstrating a tangible increase. Although He had a rate of attrition (or falling away), He was able to show evidence of how His mentoring significantly affected those who were left. At the day of Pentecost, there were 102 in the room waiting to receive their upper level staff development.

The parable of the talents also demonstrates that we will be held accountable for more than just what we receive. We will be evaluated according to what we *do* with what we have.

Sustain-ability is having and demonstrating the ability to continue providing support and development for your organization through diverse and effective resource and revenue development activities. Learning Goal: Learn about types of contributions and partnerships to consider for donor and resource development.

Sustainability efforts provide the ability to continue the program beyond the grant amount that is awarded by a funder or donors. Organizations should carefully consider alternatives to funding and even work performance with a reduced staff. There is no way of knowing for certain that funds that have even been promised will absolutely become available when scheduled. This is especially true with government funds.

However even private and corporate donors need to know that an organization is looking to them for support and is not solely dependent upon their contributions for existence. Funders want to know that they are not the only source of funds that is being used by an organization. They want to know that the organization has the support of the community as well as other donors.

In every Request for Proposal (RFP) that our organization has responded to, we have been asked about our plans to sustain. There is generally a point system that helps to determine if an applicant ranks high enough to receive the grant award. The ability to sustain a project is generally a high ranking category.

It makes sense to donors that an organization that began without a particular donor would plan on being able to sustain in the event that a donor could no longer continue to provide financial assistance. Financial assistance can be halted for a number of reasons. For example a donor may die suddenly without having made provisions for a project or program that may have even been favored. However the organization has to deal with the reality that the funds simply stopped coming after the donor is deceased.

Some other unfortunate instances that may occur include an economic influence that reduces the amount of giving overall. Often when the economy becomes questionable or unstable, philanthropists make significant reductions in their giving.

Partnerships That Help You to Sustain

A secret to sustaining is partnering with other organizations that will add your proposal contents to theirs. If you can make their proposals more compelling with what you bring to the table, they will want to keep collaborating with you.

You can also get funded through Agreements where you provide services for organizations that have been issued grant awards. Use the resources in this book to find funded organizations that might need the services that you offer. Send them a letter explaining your experience and that you would be willing to complete your portion of your proposal.

Using this strategy allowed me to help raise millions of dollars for my students. I recognized through my own experience that collaborative projects are much more attractive for a number of reasons. One of the main reasons that collaborations are good investments is that each entity has its own connection and resources.

The leaders of other organizations are also social entrepreneurs. As social entrepreneurs they are accustomed to taking risks. They are not like employees who are simply interested in a paycheck. They are stakeholders who recognize that supporting your efforts will make it easier for them to gain their own success.

As you continue to seek God about how you will build your own outreach efforts, remember to start with the community that houses your facility. Even if you do not have a separate church building, still focus on the neighborhood where you live. But remain ready to reach the *world* through the access that technology offers using the internet.

Remember to offer specialized services and support according to the struggles that you have personally overcome. And also make sure that you mentor followers in love, faith and service so that your ministry can remain a legacy for years to come.

Jesus taught His disciples how to gain access to the Father and gave them the Holy Spirit to provide power to increase. Jesus established the structure of succession and increase through discipleship. He also inspired extra support by promoting and producing good results. Because of His good works and those of His disciples, others offered to support them by their own means. He even sent additional help to the disciples (Paul). Jesus also prepared His followers to partake of His own increase ("I go to prepare a place for you").

I believe that all visionaries should take note of the model of succession planning that Jesus demonstrated. We need to make sure that we have documented a plan that can be followed long after we leave this earth or are unable to have direct influence over the operations of our program, ministry, etc.

The Faith Connection to Social Services- 68 -

Jesus is our best example of how to establish effective social services. In order to continue the legacy of his mission to save souls and sustain, Jesus recruited servants that He called his disciples. Knowing that He would need workers to teach others Jesus began succession planning from the start of His ministry. The thoroughness of His indoctrination would later greatly contribute to the sustainability of His initiative.

Some examples of social services include: homeless shelters, employment services, community food distribution, after school programs and substance abuse intervention. Many people prefer to use faith-based social services that churches are establishing such as community health centers and elderly care centers. For practically every societal ill, there is a need for assistance that also comforts those who are suffering.

Jesus reinforced essential organizational values. He continued to teach and emphasize that the greatest among them would be those that serve. His teaching was a combination of information as well as demonstration. Jesus declared that even He came to serve and proceeded to demonstrate his own service. He let his disciples know that the one that they were following and referring to as LORD and Master was also a servant.

Jesus taught that a servant is no greater than the master. Therefore all those who claim to follow Jesus should also learn to become service providers. Jesus establishes our faith connection to social services.

My initial studies caused me to be inundated with so much information that it was difficult to find a starting place to teach those Pastors who wanted to learn about mainstream philanthropy.

The R.A.T.E.S.™ development concepts were produced in response to the need to provide a consistent standard of development and practice. It also proved to serve as a method to connect faith community leaders with social entrepreneurship.

Our needs assessments revealed a prominent concern regarding time availability that challenged ministry leaders. We also found that certain denominations that had less focus upon biblical studies were less receptive to learning how to engage their congregations with mainstream philanthropy. Yet we were still encouraged with anticipating the tremendous good that could be accomplished if more grassroots church leaders were empowered with social entrepreneurship skills and resources.

The R.A.T.E.S. Principles offer a universal standard of operations to help build strategies. They also assist with building effective tools to allow churches to work together to truly impact lives and communities.

Chapter Six **Developing a Program**

- *The Faith Based Initiative*
- *Faith Friendly Government Funds*
- *Planning Activities for Objectives*

Jesus had a definite organizational structure that could be modeled by all of his followers. Many of today's non-profit organizations also follow this model.

This model includes: having and expressing a vision, rationale for the vision, mission, goals and objectives. The points below describe how Jesus operated in this model:

- Vision (Broad yet provable): To save people from sin and death

- Rationale: People have been sinning without understanding what sin is and that it destroys life. They also do not understand that sin separates them from the God who gives life, love, joy and wealth. They also do not know how to atone for their sins in order to make peace with God and acquire eternal life, love, joy and wealth.

- Mission (ongoing): To preach the gospel to the poor, heal the broken hearted, set at liberty those who are captive, preach recovery of sight to the blind.

- Goal (Measurable and Provable): to establish a church that will develop disciples to preach the gospel to all of the nations, teaching people how to be saved.

- Objectives (Measurable and provable): 1) Recruit 12 Apostles 2) Mentor 12 disciples 3) Perform # miracles 4) Preach the gospel to 4,000 5) Heal 5 sick 6) Cast out 7 demons 6)die on the cross 7) Arise from the dead 8) Establish a church 9) Commission the 12 disciples

Today, the world has embraced the model that Jesus practiced as a required standard. Unfortunately, the church at large has not so readily adopted this structure as a standard for organizational operations. Hopefully, the need for this type of structure will find its way into the hearts of the faith community leadership.

There was a federally funded program called Access to Recovery that we were able to study using the R.A.T.E.S.™ principles. We found that it offered much success by collaborating with faith based and community organizations along with public agencies. Although there were some challenges, we found that using R.A.T.E.S.™ development principles, faith based organizations, new to government funded programs, could perform well with providing tangible social services.

The Department of Substance Abuse and Mental Health Services Administration was the administrator of this grant program. The following description of this program comes directly from their site:
President Bush announced in his 2003 State of the Union Address a new substance abuse treatment initiative, Access to Recovery. This new initiative will provide people seeking drug and alcohol treatment with vouchers to pay for a range of appropriate community-based services.

Congress has appropriated $100 million in both the 2004 and 2005 budget for the Substance Abuse and Mental Health Services Administration (SAMHSA) to launch the initiative. After a competitive grant process that reviewed applications from 44 states and 22 tribes and territories, funds were awarded to 14 states and one tribal organization: California, Connecticut, Florida, Idaho, Illinois, Louisiana, Missouri, New Jersey, New Mexico, Tennessee, Texas, Washington, Wisconsin, Wyoming, and the California Rural Indian Health Board, to implement Access to Recovery.

The Administration's commitment to expand clinical treatment and recovery support services to reach those in need extends beyond the immediate fiscal year, with its FY 2006 request to increase Access to Recovery's appropriation to $150 million.

The problem that this program was to address focused on abuse of alcohol and illicit drug use. This program also stated the specific outcomes that would be used to measure the degree of success. These outcomes included: abstinence from drugs and alcohol; along with attainment of employment or enrollment in school, no involvement with the criminal justice system; stable housing; social support; access to after care; and retention in services.

The combination of outcomes already established a challenge for success, because the outcomes were not all clearly related to the stated problem. In fact the additional required outcomes were often direct challenges to achieving the primary outcome, which was abstinence from drugs and alcohol. For example, unstable housing challenged the ability to administer consistent services in order to yield positive results.

Because participating agencies had to include the outcome of employment and stable housing, there was always the challenge of partners leaning more towards achieving those objectives while losing sight of the primary problem. For instance, even though a job such as telemarketing provided a paycheck, the stress of needing to meet quotas may have contributed to a relapse back into using drugs.

Some common results that remained *under* the radar included participants becoming ill because the stress also decreased the ability to fight off sickness. The doctor then prescribed medication that caused the type of sensation or feelings that were once experienced by the illicit drugs or alcohol. This may not test positive in a drug screening, but will rekindle the desire for the feeling that was once provided by the drugs or alcohol. This revisiting of those feelings often resulted in relapse of illicit drug related activities.

On the other hand, those who were not pressured to obtain employment or housing tended to be less likely to relapse while on their path to recovery. We found that the agencies responded to the pressure of delivering the outcomes by pressuring the *clients* to produce the outcomes. And eliminating the primary problem became meshed in the mix of other problems that were related to the outcome requirements.

Perhaps, if the primary problem of illicit drug or alcohol use had been identified as the *sole* problem that was being addressed, the participating agencies could have planned more targeted efforts. The lesson that we learn is that an attempt to address too many problems simultaneously, using the same resources, greatly hinders success and generates wasted efforts. It also risks false assessments for success that deter necessary responses to lingering problems.

For example, once a participant has been assessed and has been tested for drugs, this person may still be counted as a success. Some have gotten employment and remained abstinent for the initial 30 to 90 days. However, the pressures of work and having to pay bills and maintain a household began to cause stress.

Since many of the programs did not cover participants for more than 90 days, the participants did not have continued access to the support system that helped to maintain sobriety. Because the agency needed to cover overhead costs, they had to maintain a flow of new clients that were still billable. The mere reality of space prohibited old clients from returning to the same facility that helped them because there was not enough room to service them.

The staff compensation was another issue that had to be considered. Salaries, space and resources were all paid for according to the number of clients served that were still billable. This left agencies with a dilemma of juggling the desire to help clients to eliminate their problem of drug or alcohol use along with the need to cover costs to provide the essential services to produce the required outcomes.

There is a difference between a problem and the root of the problem. Many people try to dig into the root causes of a problem in order to develop solutions, but the root causes of an initial problem may no longer be an issue to the one who is suffering.

For example, someone struggling with substance abuse was counseled by a worker who had uncovered that the client was from a physically abusive household. The prescribed treatment was targeted towards addressing physical as well as substance abuse. However, the client when counseled by another expressed that a relapse occurred after being distraught over the recent death of a loved one. The worker who chose to address grief counseling was significantly more successful with causing the client to feel a sense of hope which led to abstinence from drug usage.

In a separate situation one of my students, (I will refer to as Tess), decided that she wanted to set up a non-profit organization to offer scholarships to single mothers. She first identified the lack of scholarships for single mothers as the problem that she wanted to address. However, upon closer examination, she found that most of the women that she wanted to help were not ready to attend college. Among her challenges included the following: 1) Women were concerned with working to care for their families 2) Many of the women had not yet received a high school diploma or GED.

Through a basic needs assessment, Tess also uncovered that most of the women did not view the lack of scholarships for college as a primary problem. Tess was challenged because all of her reasons for developing her non-profit foundation rested upon her perception that scholarships would be a solution to the problem. But what was really the problem?

As our sessions progressed, we uncovered that the problem which really concerned Tess was a lack of the ability to acquire gainful employment. She reasoned that the lack of college education was the problem that contributed to the inability to get adequate employment. She pointed out that her own college education was what afforded her the opportunity to acquire and maintain gainful employment.

Tess learned that people seldom have one problem that needs to be addressed. Most problematic situations are attached to other problems. Many of the women would not be able to take advantage of the scholarships that she offered for various reasons. Some needed daycare. Some needed encouragement and confidence that they could obtain a degree. Some would need tutoring because they had poor study habits. Tess was not prepared nor interested in addressing these other needs. Still, she was able to recognize that these factors could affect the results of her efforts. I encouraged her to do some research to find other organizations that could offer help in the areas that were uncovered in her needs assessment.

It is difficult to develop a program until you first settle upon which of the needs you will address and then plan who can partner with to address other essential needs. Based upon this understanding you can, determine your goals and objectives for eliminating the problem according to the needs.

"Planting Good Works to Produce Good Fruit"

Chapter Seven Funds & Resources

- *The Faith-Based Initiative*
- *Faith Friendly Government Funds*
- *Overcoming a Lack of Resources*

The Faith-Based Initiative

There is much misinformation about what many refer to as *the faith-based initiative*. Many people have incorrectly told people that if you receive government funds then the government will try to shut you down. The government could shut you down whether you receive government grants or not. Government grants are made up of funds from tax payers including me and you as well as foreign or domestic businesses. These funds have been set aside to provide resources for non-profit and even for-profit organizations that are willing to provide needed social and human services. These grants allow people within the community to be a part of the solution for their own issues.

As president of the United States of America, George Bush signed an executive order intended to eliminate the discrimination against government funds going to the faith community for providing social and community services. However the initial door was opened in 1996 by former President Bill Clinton with Charitable Choice. Moving forward, the newly elected president, Barrack Obama also promotes the benefits of embracing a Faith-based initiative.

It is true that there have been churches that have gotten in trouble after receiving government funds. But the situation is generally caused by their non-compliance to the conditions of the contract. For example, the payroll that was budgeted to include taxes and fringe benefits should result in paid taxes. Many funded churches did not understand that they had to actually pay taxes from their grant award for the workers according to the proposed budget. Additionally, if the contract states that you are going to service 100 clients, then you cannot (for example) expect to get paid the same compensation for servicing 25 clients.

With so many churches setting up spaces in communities across the nation, why are so many people still looking to the government to meet their needs? Before there was welfare, there were churches with congregations that practiced helping those who were in need. Before Temporary Assistance for Needy Families (TANF), there were church members that took responsibility for giving to the poor. Before Aid for Dependent Children (ADC) and homeless programs, there were church members that looked after widows and orphans and took in those needing shelter. Before Link cards there were mission minded believers that made it their responsibility to feed the hungry.

Over the years the complacency of the faith community as a whole allowed the world to get the glory for doing what believers are called to do. For example, the youth in desperate need for protection from child molesters have gotten the most vocalized support from every day citizens protesting child abuse. However, in today's faith community, too many church leaders all but ignore this critical issue.

Faith Friendly Government Funds

There are a number of church leaders who avoid obtaining a tax exempt status because they feel that it invites government scrutiny. A non-profit status allows organizations to have access to tax breaks as somewhat of a means of relieving the financial burdens that exist with service providers. Additionally, those who contribute to your cause may enjoy filing tax deductions that decrease their tax liability.

These tax deductions help decrease the financial obligation of those who help the world by contributing to socially viable tax-exempt programs. These contributors are rewarded for relieving the financial burden of operating a non-profit organization. Churches that refuse to obtain a tax-exempt status deprive their contributors of maximum tax breaks. By the way, anyone's books can be audited if impropriety is suspected. This includes churches.

I believe that God is positioning church leadership to receive resources in order to provide fair and wise distribution to those who need it. Likewise, a growing number of church leaders are daring to require their congregations to be proactive in providing for the communities where their sanctuary or church facility is located. Churches are establishing charitable organizations to address the needs of the community while offering hope for a better future.

Overcoming a Lack of Resources

Paul makes a statement in the Bible about being content "whether abase or abound." He teaches that his relationship with God was the source of his pleasure and contentment. Because of this mindset, if He lacked in material resources, He was not paralyzed from continuing to do God's work.

As social servants, we have to learn how to adopt this same mindset. There will be times that money and resources are scarce. This scarcity can be quite challenging, especially if others depend on you for their income. One of the tests of whether you are working with the right staff is seeing their efforts to help the program to sustain when money is tight. I learned that it is important to brace myself to endure the financial storms rather than always work to avoid them.

We had people working with us that proved their dedication with their commitment to continue even after the checks stopped. For the Access to Recovery project, we had decided to mentor and hire as many recovering clients as possible. Many of them had not ever had such an opportunity before working with us. We exposed them to much of the same training that the other staff experienced. Of course we made mistakes in giving access and even responsibility. However in the long run we found committed workers who were invaluable assets when things got rough.

The lack of resources needed to sustain adequate staff is certainly among the most challenging aspects of running a social service program. Fortunately, the fact that we were a faith-based organization allowed us to rely on faith in God to take us beyond our challenges. We were able to turn to God for strength, guidance and favor. Only God kept us from quitting. If we had quit we would have denied ourselves the opportunity to know what we can handle with God's help. We made it through the storms because God was our shelter.

Actually the lack of resources taught us how to be more frugal with our spending. Consequently, our budgets also reflected more accountability. We became acutely aware and appreciative of bargains and resource management. This positioned us to demonstrate how well we would be able to manage the funds and resources that God wanted to provide for us through the generosity of others.

The best way to plan for resources is to make sure that the resources directly connect with the stated goals and objectives. Your staff, along with all financial and material resources should reflect how you are going to make life better for your target population. When donors can clearly see this connection, they will want to make sure that you have the support needed to succeed.

"Planting Good Works to Produce Good Fruit"

Chapter Eight Recruiting Stakeholders

- *The Churches Challenge with Anonymity*
- *Getting Congregational Involvement*
- *No Excuses*

The Churches Challenge with Anonymity

In 1964 newspapers reported that as many as 38 people were aware of a particular crime being committed, but did not respond. Sometime after 2:00 AM a woman was brutally stabbed and raped. The reports would include one person who turned up his television to drown out the screams.

This was one of the tragic incidents that prompted psychologists to begin researching a phenomenon known as "diffusion of responsibility." They were looking to understand how people could be non-responsive to the cries for help of others. Their research would explore how people could be aware of someone being victimized and do nothing.

Many people in the church may be victims as well as practitioners of this "bystander effect." In psychology, the bystander effect is a term which declares that people appear to be less likely to help someone when there are more people around. This may help explain why people flock to large church congregations to remain anonymous and distant from other church members.

Unfortunately, this anonymity has contributed to the perception of the church being weak and purposeless in the eyes of the world. Too many church members have demonstrated complacency regarding the works of the ministry. Many may even reason that because they are not doing "bad" they are not responsible for "doing good". However the Bible reads in James 4:17 that, "Therefore to him that knoweth to do good, and doeth it not, to him it is sin."

Getting Congregational Involvement

Church members need to be taught how to serve as stakeholders. When they understand that they have a real stake or benefit with the survival and growth of a ministry, they will gladly contribute all they can. These stakeholders have much to offer because God has gifted them for the works of the ministry. Unfortunately the church leadership has not been able to tap into these resources by empowering their membership to act as stakeholders.

In today's churches the leadership is often a one-man or one-woman show. Even though there may be others with leadership titles, they are often the "amen corner." They merely encourage and agree with what the Pastor has already decided to do. This type of support deprives the Pastor of the accountability that is truly needed in order to be successful.

Our Lord Jesus is the ideal model for organizational development that produces a lasting legacy. And with all the power that Jesus possessed, He still assembled support staff. The example that Jesus set was one that began with his own personal development and networking with others in an exchange of information and ideas. He would go to the temples and market places and anywhere that He could speak to a gathering of people. Then He gathered his support system of twelve disciples.

Although Jesus was the central earthly figure, His disciples were expected to provide services as well. After He secured his primary staff, Jesus continued with staff development that consisted of personal mentoring. An ideal mentor is one who teaches while nurturing someone through the practical application of what is being taught. Jesus demonstrated what his followers would be doing. He did not simply tell them what to do.

Jesus also explained the rationale for why they would be doing what He showed them. All of the workers were not given all of the same instruction. However all of them were given reinforcement about the primary mission along with the primary activities and attitude that would be expected of them. This encouraged the disciples to act according to purpose and passion rather than simply go through the motions.

Churches populated by members who are just going through the motions, have to coerce people to give to sustain the ministry. I have heard many Pastors insist that they have to only rely on tithes offerings and the usual efforts to raise dollars and resources just to keep the church going. The usual efforts that churches use to raise funds often include: bake sales, raffles, special offering requests, anniversary celebrations and even revivals.

For the most part, the contributions come from the same people. The regular congregation may accept the times when asked to dig a little deeper in order to give a little more. Those who can afford to give more may at times need to experience some additional motivation to give what they could have given from the beginning.

Many of today's churches are frequented by attendees who once showed up at a service hoping for some answers or solutions to their problems. Their unanswered questions have led them to stop expecting that the church is relevant to their real and tangible problems. Therefore instead of expecting solutions from the church many people look to other sources such as books, television, advice columns, the internet, etc. Unfortunately, these sources tap into the finances that could have been contributed to church based solutions.

For many, their hope has simply deteriorated to acceptance. They accept that the church cannot help them to get rid of their problems. They accept that the church is only supposed to be motivational but not very relevant. This acceptance has planted seeds of complacency which gives birth to restlessness and anxiousness.

You can see this restlessness and preoccupation in action during the church services. People are looking around daydreaming while anxiously wanting to move on to more enjoyable pursuits. I have been in conversations with people who admitted to saying "Amen" in church to statements they didn't understand or even hear.

Even church leaders are finding themselves reviewing their own lives and scratching their heads wondering if they are doing the right thing. It is a scary thing to examine your life and feel that you have wasted most of it. For believers, the confidence of eternal life may be hindered by the fear of having to answer to God for the deeds done while in the body. The bible teaches us that those who know the good to do and do not do it are sinning. (James 4:17)

A growing number of faith community leaders are making the decision to be about their Father's business by setting up community outreach projects. Their projects are being used to demonstrate God's love in action. They are determined to produce good fruit.

Following Jesus is not just about the things that you *stop* doing. It is not enough to *stop* fornicating or *stop* cheating or *stop* stealing. You can still be in sin by not *doing* the *good* that you ought to be doing. When you do the good that you are called and anointed to do, you demonstrate true religion and compassion that comes from the love of God.

Imagine our world with a common practice that our children are taught to contribute to the good of others. Now imagine that faith leaders encouraged and taught their congregations to practice collaborative philanthropy —even joining efforts with other congregations. Imagine how much better the world could be.

This is not about common religion, but about true religion which is looking after widows and orphans. This is not about expanding church membership, but rather about practicing Christ's commission of discipleship. A disciple is a mentor that remains in learning mode as a follower and servant of the Master who commissions him or her. Imagine that type of personal involvement by faith leaders.

What do you think would happen if churches all over the globe agreed to pool their congregational resources to address the pain and suffering in their communities? I mean if they decided to work together to go beyond the weekly worship services and bible studies and used their facilities to provide much needed human and social services such as learning centers, arts & cultural development, clinics, after school programs, substance abuse recovery support groups and elderly daycare projects.

You might say that you know some churches that are doing these things already. You might even lead or attend such a church. But I am talking about churches working together to *maximize* their impact in the community by joining their resources. You might then say that this sounds great but it will *never* happen. However, this is exactly what's happening with a growing number of churches and faith community leaders.

This book describes an example of a model that includes churches, community, businesses and public service agencies working together to serve a specific target population. The project described in Chapter Six is a federally funded initiative called Access to Recovery. The participating faith-based service providers learned how to develop projects that have received funds, resources and support to truly make a difference. They experienced what could happen when churches join their resources to provide social services.

I believe that we learn by our challenges and failures even more than from doing what comes easily. The R.A.T.E.S.™ concept for development builds upon tried and tested biblical principles that lead to great success and prosperity. Godly prosperity is holistic because it also includes mental and physical fulfillment as well as spiritual healing. However the principles have to be faithfully applied even in the face of struggles.

I believe that the Lord is preparing faith community leaders to practice accountability and prudence along with compassion. I also believe that those who learn the best will be entrusted and empowered with the most. My own experience has demonstrated what can happen when someone is open and submissive to apply Godly principles while seeking to be an obedient servant of the Lord.

No Excuses- 94 -

It is easy to blame others and circumstances for our failure to go forward in charitable service. I once blamed my Pastor for hindering me from operating in my "anointing" and call to ministry. This is not an acceptable defense to use with Jesus at judgment. Remember that the scriptures teach that we will still have to give an account for everything done while in the body. We will not be able to say, "Wait a minute Almighty God, while I get my Pastor to tell you how I was hindered from obeying you."

We know when we are just using our Pastor or boss, politicians, spouse or even our parents, children and others as an excuse to mask our real fears of failure. We need to believe that we have a (God given) ability to move forward with what we have been called and chosen to accomplish. Even if we do not accomplish all that we hoped, it does not automatically mean that we failed. However we set ourselves up for failure if we refuse to follow the appropriate guidelines.

It is my conviction that all believers are called to social and human service by Jesus because all believers are called to follow Jesus as His disciple. Jesus provided social and human services on His way to the cross. He fed the hungry, healed the sick and encouraged the broken hearted. But Jesus recruited disciples that He taught and commissioned to also provide social and human services. This demonstrated that His works were not only for prophets, preachers and pastors. Jesus empowered and sent out common people of various backgrounds.

Mother Fort (who is mentioned in Chapter One of this book) is my biological mother. She taught me to love and serve the Lord wholeheartedly. She also told me that I will always be cut off from the fullness of my blessings until I started operating in the area of ministry that God has called me.

I gave Mother Fort many excuses about why I felt that I was hindered in my abilities to operate in ministry. But I soon realized that my mother was right- again. All I had to do was ask. God had already prepared the way for others to respond favorably to my requests. Being a service provider has opened so many doors for me and also made me a continuous recipient of God's provisions.

At first I was acting as a service provider but then I declared my decision to walk in my calling as a service provider. As I went forward for the sake of discipleship, I started to see significant growth in power, wisdom and favor.

I had often wondered how the Bible could express an existence where someone would be "complete, not lacking anything." But I have realized that our God is our source to uncommon fulfillment. He teaches us that we can be blessed with peace of mind and fullness of joy. Additionally, the holy scriptures also reveal that God blesses His people with earthly treasures and "adds no sorrow to it."

I believe that there are those who have the skill and expertise to acquire great wealth to empower others for the works of the ministry. The scriptures teach that Jesus and the disciples were supported financially by those that believed in what they were doing and could afford to support them. Even small amounts by large numbers can accumulate sufficient resources to accomplish great deeds.

It seems as though by the time church leaders are willing to take the time to explore obtaining resources from other areas than just tithes and offerings, they are in a state of emergency. Usually something is about to get cut off or repossessed or closed down. Sometimes this is what it takes to get the attention that was being sought before, but ignored due to busyness.

At the point that the church leader agrees to try something different, it is still uncertain as to how much effort will be committed. The precious commodity of time is closely guarded and only given with much scrutiny. Many church leaders prioritize their availability according to which engagements will net the highest short term return. They tend to participate in activities that promise immediate reward much more often than those that involve planning for a secure future.

The concentration on quick return activities may account for why few Pastors have a legal tax exempt status. The time, effort and money needed to prepare the appropriate documentation simply conflicts with the more urgent demands of ministry. Likewise, the cost and communications needed to file for tax exempt status appears to be a luxury that may be approached sometime after the ministry is doing better and is more stable.

One day, the Pastor that put off obtaining proper certification and legal status may realize that this investment would have better positioned the church to gain valuable resources. The good news is that more faith leaders are stepping up to the plate and realigning their values with what it takes to have a successful ministry.

A successful ministry is one that is holistic in the services that are being provided. It is also one that connects the believers and followers with the overall mission of Jesus as members of the whole body of Christ. A successful ministry is one that sustains itself and seeks ways to offer support for other ministries that may be struggling. The works of a successful ministry help to make disciples of Jesus who are dedicated to advancing the kingdom of God.

The door of empowerment leads to a storehouse of resources with access to spacious rooms of opportunity for growth and expansion. Empowerment is a term that defines the act of providing strength and energy. A person who feels empowered will have the strength and energy to go after and receive resources that are needed. The right resources increase access to opportunities. There is no growth or expansion without adequate opportunities to promote them.

Preparing for resources is about more than what you do. It is about first knowing what you are and what you can offer. For example a person may operate or function as an administrator, but not truly be an administrator. This person will more likely fall short of initiating and completing tasks that a true administrator performs instinctively.

Another person may operate as the Chief Executive Officer (CEO) of an organization simply because he or she thought about the idea to establish a project. However all visionaries are not necessarily called to be organizers or to lead a project.

Some people are planters, some are laborers and others may be harvesters. People should be careful not to use up their efforts and resources inappropriately by trying to operate outside of their duties and responsibilities. People who are not familiar with an area of functionality tend to delegate resources according to their limited knowledge. The misuse or improper use of resources reduces the quality and fullness of results.

If a planter becomes preoccupied with laboring, he or she burdens the energy and resources for laboring that should be applied to successful planting. In other words, that person will use the energy that was intended for planting on labor related activities. This will lessen the success of their true call to plant. Likewise, a laborer that decides that it is time to try to harvest something will upset the abundance of fruitfulness that is intended with skillful and timely harvesting.

The results of operating outside of a call to duty include falling short of the intended success. The outcome that could have been achieved will be limited and sometimes dangerously hindered. In short, people operating outside of their calling cause deficiencies in production. They do this by wasting the resources that they lack passion and skills to use.

I strongly believe that the ministries that operate according to what is taught in this book will experience the great benefits of having stakeholders among their congregations. They will prosper beyond their imagination because of the great favor that is multiplied through empowering those stakeholders who are working with them.

I was amazed at how God used others to contribute to our sustaining after we began to apply the principles described in this book. God sent people to hold us up in prayer as well as give to us materially. Even our family and social relationships grew in how they blessed us. We began to experience a peace and enjoyment with each other that I had not even thought to hope for.

As long as we are able to treat others as stakeholders, we will know what it is to have valuable support. A crucial key is to also *serve* as a stakeholder for *others*.

"Planting Good Works to Produce Good Fruit"

Chapter Nine **Real World Experiences With Grant Proposals**

- *Getting Our Feet Wet*
- *Handling the Rejection Letter*
- *The Purpose and Nature of a Grant Proposal*
- *Reducing Proposal Writing Stress*
- *The Difference Between Grant Writing and Proposal Writing*
- *What it Takes to Be a Good Grant Proposal Writer*
- *Basics for Writing a Grant Proposal*
- *Telling the Truth About Abilities*
- *Engaging Technology*
- *Demonstrate Your Use of Technology*
- *A Reason why Your Tax Exempt Status is Not Enough to Get a Grant*
- *How to Get Non-profit Donations without Having Your Own 501 (c) (3) Tax Exempt Status*

Getting Our Feet Wet

The tension was high and tempers were agitated. The clock was typically uncooperative as it warned us that the hands of time were waving good bye. Good bye to the opportunity to get $450,000 in grant funds to run our program. We knew that if we did not assemble our proposal package and send it off in the next few minutes that all of our efforts would have been wasted.

There had been three of us scrambling to complete our $450,000 document. Our newfound friend who convinced us to apply for the grant in the first place was working feverishly with Rev. Dr. Aaron Jamal, (my husband) and me. "Just put the copies together," I anxiously demanded while plundering through the piles of printed discards that were scattered across the table, desk and floor.

I was determined that this proposal was going to arrive on time and in fact if I had to drive to the airport and personally book it on a FedEx flight. I had not heard of

²And the LORD answered me, and said, Write the vision, and make it plain upon tables, that he may run that readeth it. ³For the vision is yet for an appointed time, but at the end it shall speak, and not lie: though it tarry, wait for it; because it will surely come, it will not tarry.

Hab 2:2 - 3 (KJV)

doing that before, but I was desperate. My mind was swirling with frantic concoctions to ensure that our proposal was submitted on time.

My husband and I were busily making some order of the 45 page document that required five copies with one original. We were not exactly sure what that meant so we simply made all of the copies alike. We decided that it would be safest for us to make each copy as complete as an original. That way the readers will not have to search for which one was the original.

We tried to make our proposal easy to read and compelling enough to receive an award. I had included a table of contents with nice page numbers. I even added attractive tables and shaded headings to make each category stand out. Our friend who worked for the state's Department of Health and Human Services helped us to develop our ideas for the proposal. She had given us many specifics to consider that I would not have included without her. I was so impressed with our proposal that I was already planning how to spend the money.

Finally after months of waiting, I had gotten the notice that we had been anxious to receive. But the contents did not read as I had hoped or expected. Everything else around me went fuzzy as I began reading, "Thank you for submitting your proposal. However"...blah blah blah and so forth.

I could hardly believe what I was reading. We had done all of that work for weeks only to get a "thanks, but no thanks" letter from the government. They must not have known how much work went into putting that entire document together. They could not possibly imagine how this whole ordeal sucked up weeks of our lives from our family and friends. Whoever signed the letter had to be totally oblivious to all of the research, office supplies, travel and postage that went into our efforts to submit a quality package.

Handling the Rejection Letter

Tears of disappointment blurred my vision as I read and re-read my first grant proposal rejection letter. I even checked to see if the letter and envelope were really addressed to us. It could have been delivered to us by mistake. As I re-examined the entire document, I realized that there were comments from readers that actually explained why our proposal was rejected.

I was sure that I could poke gaping holes in the reviewers' assessments of our well prepared documentation. The reviewers' comments pointed out our proposal's lack of detail regarding just how we were going to carry out our plan. The critics actually had the nerve to mention our lack of evidence that we had the ability to deliver results according the plan that we proposed.

The reviewers' critique of our proposal was the first time that I met with the term which would haunt me for years. This term was "capacity." One of the reviewers wrote that we did not demonstrate having the capacity to do what we had proposed. After reading this admonishment I was sure that I had not properly introduced them to the dynamic duo of my husband and myself.

The Jamal Team would be the Executive Director, Program Manager, Project Director, Technicians, and more. We knew that we could do this because this is how we were functioning already. Of course we passed out at the end of the day. But we had backup. Our four children were drafted into our whirlwind preoccupations. We were merely broadening their perspectives. We made them our unwitting assistants whenever necessary- which was quite often.

I began combing through a copy of our proposal to start building my case to challenge the reviewers' assessments. However, somewhere guarded securely by my fractured pride, my discernment agreed with what I read.

A few years later, I realized that I was definitely fortunate not to have gotten funded. This may sound strange, but I am grateful, because I probably would have faced a lesson that would still haunt me. I probably would have gotten in trouble for mismanagement among other things.

What would have happened if we had gotten the grant is that we would have been over burdened and still under funded. One significant difference with running over worked without grant funding is having the ability to cut back your hours and responsibility if needed. However a funded grant proposal commits the awarded organization to specific duties and obligations. These requirements cannot be filed in a "to be continued-maybe" category.

A Lesson about Problems

Today I can say, "thank you Lord for sparing us from receiving that first grant." This may seem strange but we could have gotten involved in something that was actually outside of our area of expertise- and anointing. This is generally a perfect setting for failure.

One of the earliest lessons that I began to learn is that every problem is not for me to solve. I am not sure how or why it began, but I would hear about problems that I took on as my responsibility to seek solutions. What made it difficult for me to resist the problem solving mode was that I was generally successful with finding effective solutions.

A dear friend of mine, Midge Lansat finally helped me understand that I was over functioning. I also realized that it made me appear to be a control hound. I was only trying to *help*. But my helping often over burdened myself and my reluctantly obliging family.

This lesson that "every problem is not for me to solve" was coupled with "just because I *could* do something did not mean that I *should* do something." I am sure to get more than a few "Amens" in agreement with that statement. I may also get a few "well wait a minute" type thoughts from others. After all we have heard it said that "the way for bad people to prosper is for good people to do nothing." I am not saying that we should simply remain unresponsive to a critical need. I am only pointing out that the most effective responses will be the ones that were carried out by those who are most capable of delivering the best results.

I have occasionally wondered why Jesus did not simply stand at the top of the highest mountain, stretch out his hands and say, "every body in the world - be healed." I truly believe that Jesus could do this and that all suffering from sickness would end at that instant. But as I learned more about the purpose of human development on earth, I realized that if Jesus took away all of the pain and suffering on earth, many of us would be robbed of the opportunity and responsibility that is developing us for our next level of existence.

This concept may be hard for many to grasp because it appears that God simply allows people to suffer unnecessarily. But I have come to accept that God has a perspective on life that I could not possibly have unless He allowed me to have it. I am convinced that the mind of God has to be far too advanced for me to reason why or how He operates. So as I look to the source that explains God to me in a way that I believe that I can understand, I find that God is just and fair and far more caring about those who suffer than I will ever be. And since God can step in and change things whenever He wants, who am I to say that I do not approve of His timing?

Many outreach oriented people like me are *doers*. We want to *do* something about a problem that really bothers us. We are natural "wanna be" problem solvers. This mindset is further complicated by having the ability to actually do a number of tasks well.

You may ask, "What is wrong with wanting to help where you can make a difference?" What is wrong is that the constant pull of new problems can greatly interfere with fulfilling the true calling that God has ordained. When people operate in what they have been anointed to do, there is a certainty of success. With each success comes an awareness that the journey and efforts are on the correct path. There is also a sense of nearing a state of completion- not lacking anything.

On the journey to completeness, there is no space for emptiness or time for regrets. There are many doers that fill empty. I believe that this emptiness is the result of not connecting with what they were intended to accomplish. My understanding about the importance of operating in one's calling began to sprout with my first serious effort to produce a government grant proposal.

When I was working on my first grant proposal, I plunged into the project with great determination. At that time, I was applying for a grant to address HIV/AIDS among youth. I knew close to nothing at all about HIV/AIDS, but as a Youth Program Director I was concerned about it hurting young people.

Our new found friend from the Colorado Department of Health and Human Services who had come to speak at our facility was quite impressed with our youth program. As the Youth Program Director, I had initiated a program called, "When Young People Talk." The program was birthed out of my desperation to find something for youth to do that would also help my own biological children. I had a rapport with the youth in our program and was able to get them to share their primary concerns which included anxieties regarding their sexuality.

Our visitor was impressed with how we addressed the issues with research as well as offered thoughtful responses to the youth participants' tough and challenging questions. We also practiced empowering our youth to become leaders and decision makers. Our youth were leaning how to write radio copy, along with public speaking and production skills. Our friend from the DHHS was convinced that we had the right elements to receive government grant dollars that would support the continuation and expansion of our program.

But when I read the Request for Proposal (aka RFP), I realized that the grant application was asking me about areas that I had not considered. Still, I thought that the responses that the proposal requested were important issues. I realized that I wanted to know these answers for myself.

I wanted to know how we would get youth to abstain from sexual activity. I wanted my own children to be virgins for life. It would have suited me just fine if they all remained virgins until married- even if they stayed single until they were 67 years old. So this project became personal for me.

This RFP was really challenging me. The more that I tried to answer the questions in the RFP application, the more I realized how unorganized I was. As a consequence, I found myself overwhelmed with research about HIV/AIDS among youth as well as about organizational development in general.

I was elated and anxious at the same time. I was elated to be in this wonderful learning mode while gaining practical knowledge that I knew would make me a better Program Director. However, I was anxious with the thought of operating a program that had so many aspects and technical concerns that were foreign to me.

Before I started working on the grant proposal, I had no idea about how complex HIV/AIDS was. I was also surprised at the extent of sexual activity that was being engaged by teens and children. And I knew that this was not a population that would readily respond to a "just say no" campaign.

I was not really certain about what could be done to reduce their likelihood of contracting *any* STDs including HIV/AIDS. I went to the Colorado DHHS to use their library which was stocked with information about best practices for HIV/AIDS prevention. While there, I was also referred to organizations that had previously been funded. I was learning about organizations headed by leaders that had been working in this area for years. This was when I really started becoming nervous because I was beginning to doubt my worthiness to even run the program.

However, I was encouraged to continue when I saw that there were very few organizations that had much experience with youth. There was clearly a program service gap regarding a need for relevant HIV/AIDS intervention and prevention services that targeted the youth. It meant that somebody with God's anointing had an opportunity to address this critical issue. I viewed this opening as an opportunity and mandate for my organization to handle this business. It occurred to me that this apparent service gap was waiting for Margaret Jamal (and company) to fill it.

Still after all of the research and late night proposal preparation I had to come to terms with a reality. We might have had the passion and a good idea to make a difference, but our organization was simply not ready to carry out the project. The feedback that I received from the grant reviewers revealed that my view was blurred with delusional aspirations.

About two years later, I applied and was awarded a winning city government grant proposal for a Community Development Block Grant (CDBG). I really only needed to update a previous grant proposal that had already been funded. The Executive Director and CEO were my brother and mother who had worked with my brother's daughter and wife to complete the previous proposal. This was a family project. They had worked together to put together a proposal that had been funded.

Being able to start with a winning proposal helped me to get an idea about what the city of Chicago considered to be a good grant proposal. But when I submitted the proposal, we received an award letter contingent upon making some adjustments. By the time all of the "adjustments" were completed, we had an almost new proposal with a new name. Because of the difference in the funding pool from the previous year, the bar had been raised for the reporting requirements.

There are increasing numbers of donors who are opening up to the idea of giving to faith based organizations. Many of these donors look for churches that are providing practical social services. Faith based social services are outreach ministries that improve the overall condition of society as needs are met. Research by credible sources such as Urban Institute and the Independent Sector indicate that faith-based service providers have a high rate of success.

The Purpose and Nature of a Grant Proposal

My experiences with government grant proposals taught me valuable lessons. One of my most valued lessons is about the nature and true purpose of a grant proposal. A grant proposal documents what the submitting organization plans to do about a problem. The same proposal also serves as the framework for a contract that binds the organization to complete the work that they propose.

Gaining an understanding about the nature of a proposal really began with our receiving a letter stating that we were awarded the grant, but for less money than we requested. My husband and I were really concerned about this because we had calculated how much we thought it would cost to run this particular program. My husband, who had become the budget preparation expert, had already found ways to cut costs to a bare minimum.

We even requested less money than we thought was needed in an effort to be more competitive. That was a BIG MISTAKE. Organizations should always be realistic with requesting funds that will allow them to successfully meet the goals and objectives that they plan.

But through our protest regarding the reduction in the amount awarded, we learned another lesson that was perhaps one of the greatest lessons. This lesson is that since grant proposals are contracts, they are negotiable.

Therefore since the grant award amount was reduced, we could adjust the projected outcomes accordingly. In other words if we propose a budget of $100,000 to service 100 youth and we are only awarded a grant for $80,000, then we can adjust the projected service number to 80 youth (or less). I learned how to renegotiate the projected outcomes and submit a budget revision which really helped the organization that we working for at the time. Before the contract revision, the organization would have surely fallen short of meeting their program requirements.

Basics for Writing Grant Proposals

Even in a slow economy, grants for essential social, economic, health and institutional issues are still made available. Grants are funds awarded in response to a plan submitted as a grant proposal for addressing these or other issues

While there are certain basics of writing grant proposals, the categories of required information may vary according to the type and amount of funding being requested. For example, a grant proposal that is seeking to cover costs for a bus to transport homeless people will not need all of the same type of information as one seeking funds to operate an after school program.

Many times a grant proposal will be submitted in response to a Request for Proposal (or RFP) from a funding source. The content of the RFP will influence the content of the grant proposal.

Grant proposals that are organized in sections make it easier for donors to locate the information. Every section should reinforce whatever issue is being proposed for funding. All of the responses provided in each section should clearly relate to the primary issue presented in the grant proposal.

The following briefly describes the basic sections that should be included when writing grant proposals:

Problem Statement: A Problem Statement identifies something wrong that is in urgent need of a solution. Keep in mind that the types of problems identifying significant pain, suffering or hardship for others will have the greatest chance for getting funded. For example, consider the following: There has been a 20% increase in substance abuse related arrests among juveniles between ages 18 through 24. Statistics from the XYZ Global Youth Initiative indicates that a common trigger for substance abuse among juveniles in this age range is social isolation.

The problem statement in the example above plainly identifies something wrong. It also indicates who has the problem and how much the problem is making an impact. This problem statement also suggests a root cause for the problem.
Notice that it did not have to address the totality of the problem, but only an area that may be addressed in the grant proposal.

Needs Statement: The needs statement describes a lack of resources required to solve a problem. For example, a portion of the needs statement could include: The social isolation that triggers the problem of substance abuse among juveniles between ages 18 through 24 reveals a need for developing socialization skills. There is a critical shortage of counselors who are able to teach socialization skills to this age group in our county.

There are distinct differences between problem statements and needs statements. However some RFPs may only have a heading for either one or the other. If this is the case, then it will be prudent to prepare the information for both the problem and the needs and include them under the one heading that is allowed. Even though there may not be a clear request to explain a problem or need, this information will certainly be expected in your grant proposal.

Goals: A goal is a general statement about the intent to reduce or eliminate a problem. It summarizes the answer about what the plan is to make the problem go away. For example, the goal could be to prevent youth (ages 18-24) from going to jail for substance abuse related charges.

Be aware when writing grant proposals, that each goal will include a set of objectives. When offered a grant, you will be held accountable to meet the goals and objectives that your grant proposal documented. For this reason, I strongly recommend that your first attempts in writing grant proposals should not include more than three goals.

Objectives: The steps to help meet the goals make up the objectives. These steps must be measurable so that they can be later proven. Suppose a grant proposal is using the goal given in the example contained in this document. In that case an objective could be as follows: To develop alternative sentencing options for 50 youth arrested for substance use related charges. The number of youth in this example is what will be measured. Also notice that the objective clearly connects with the stated goal.

The steps given in objectives should indicate *what* will take place or happen. There will be a detailed work plan or method describing *how* and *when* the objectives will be completed.

Program objectives require specific activities that must be done. These activities must directly result in meeting the given objectives. For example if there is an objective to hold 5 workshops about time management, one of the activities could be to design flyers to promote the workshops.

Program Activities: Activities that are not well planned are often not carried out with much success. Even an activity that appears as insignificant as preparing flyers may hinder the success of a project. If there is not enough thought about producing a flyer, the resulting appearance may be unattractive. An unattractive flyer will not draw people appropriately.

Also if the essential activity is not documented among the plans, then it may not be addressed at all. What would happen if only a few days before the workshops are to take place, someone realizes that the event has not even been adequately publicized? This happens much more than you might think.

Implementation: This section may be called different names such as "Methodology" or "Scope of Services", depending upon the type of grant or preferences of the grantor. However, the body of information is essentially the same when writing grant proposals. This section will illustrate a project design that describes a plan to meet the goals and objectives.

The implementation is the section of a grant proposal for describing what will be done and how the activities will be carried out. It will also determine the type of staffing and resources needed to make the proposed project successful. The implementation will illustrate a brief walk through of what clients or participants will actually experience when they participate in the project. The sequential activities outlined in this section should include a general timeline for when they are expected to take place or be completed.

Organizational Capacity: After the plans to reduce or eliminate a problem have been effectively described in the implementation section, the grant proposal still needs to prove that the applicant has the ability to make it happen.

This section should demonstrate that the applicant has a good idea of what it will take to run the project which includes adequate staffing and resources.

The capacity is the sufficiency of the staffing, resources etc. to make sure that the project produces favorable results. This section will also offer brief bios of the primary personnel that will be working on behalf of the organization requesting funding. Any past experience for providing related services should also be included here.

Evaluation Plan: Everyone who receives funds for their projects will be required to prove the extent their project was beneficial. The evaluation plan in a grant proposal will demonstrate "how" as well as "how much" things change for the better as a result of what was done. The evaluation plan also describes the type of information that will be collected and reported to assess the proposed effort or project.

The evaluation data will provide facts and figures about the effect on the goals, objectives and project implementation. An evaluation allows donors to have a measurable accounting of how impacting their contribution was. NOTE: I highly recommend that this portion of the grant proposal is completed with someone who understands evaluation concepts.

Budget: Many people make the mistake of using the same figures for the project budget and the organizational budget. A project budget is different from an organizational budget even though both must be considered in a grant proposal. For example, an organizational budget may include the cost for: rent, telephones, supplies and the Executive Director. On the other hand, a project budget should display only the portion of the rent, telephones, supplies and the Executive Director that is dedicated to the project.

The salary for the Executive Director is a common budgetary item where grant proposals are especially scrutinized.
In a project budget, The Executive Director should be compensated according to how much of his or her time is spent on the project. Therefore if the organization pays the Executive Director $65,000, the project budget may only allow for the percentage of time that the Executive Director will spend on the project. If this is 50% of the time, then the project budget should reflect 50% of the total (organizational) salary which is $32,5000.

Budget Narrative: A grant proposal budget needs to be complete with calculations that show how each cost was determined. This detail is summarized in a budget narrative. Budget narratives are required to offer a brief explanation about why and how money is being spent. The justification for the expenses should reflect the stated goals, objectives and project implementation

Abstract: An abstract is a summary of the project that generally includes the brief information regarding the problem, needs, overall plan, target population, cost and experience of the applicant. This synopsis is generally contained on one page and may also be used for press releases.

Executive Summary: An executive summary is a more expanded detail that may include a summary from every section in the proposal. The executive summary should be limited to between 2 and 4 pages. Both the abstract and executive summary is developed after a proposal is completed. However they are generally the first documentation that a reviewer will read.

When you are awarded a grant, the contents of your grant proposal will be used to develop the contract requirements for the money that you are given. With this in mind, your grant proposal should only include what you know you can accomplish with the amount that you are requesting.

Regardless of the grant source, your ability to receive funding will rely upon your efforts to make your case in writing. Preparing thoughtful responses to the basic sections offered in this writing will give you a good foundation for submitting a winning grant proposal.

Reducing Proposal Writing Stress

Next, I graduated to a state grant with some really good help and input from a community activist from Chicago's Westside. Her name was Ms. King. She was patient and pointed me in the right direction to learn what was needed.

We had hired a grant proposal writer who was a skilled story teller. I developed the meat and context of the proposal with Ms. King's guidance. And the grant proposal writer made it less technical and more personable. She also helped with some of the research. The greatest benefit that I received from the writer was that she gave me a sense of having additional support. This was another lesson that I learned. Even the appearance of support can make preparing a proposal less stressful.

Now let us address the stress. While this experience was not as bad as the first time with the HIV/AIDS grant proposal, it was still a nerve racking ordeal. My problem was that I found that I actually liked doing it. I still do not know why, but I enjoy doing the research and developing a program for a proposal. But the thing that makes me think that maybe I need a good therapist is that I also delight in the pressure. Just pray for me. And if you know a good "grant proposal writers anonymous" group please let me know.

This experience with Ms. King was contributed to my motivation to help others to apply for and receive grants. I wanted to help others to support their community service efforts by teaching them how to apply for the funds and resources. My own extensive search for qualified help revealed that many people who claimed the ability to develop good grant proposals really did not know how to give support to fledgling organizations.

There are a lot of individuals and organizations that offer services to help people to write grant proposals in the hope of getting money to operate their organizations. There are also a lot of people and organizations that have decided to help people to start and develop their non-profit organizations. It has been my experience along with other organizations who offer this grant development support that the leadership is unsure about what they would do with the money if they received it.

Many organizations have no idea about just how much of a problem this could be. This uncertainty also makes it difficult to produce a grant proposal that makes a good case for receiving funds. I knew from my own experience and the experience of others that a great number of people submitting grant proposals were not ready to be funded.

They often have a lot of ideas regarding what they would like to do, but their ideas are generally not well planned. This is typical because this type of thinking is not natural to many of us. When we decide to do something, we seldom stop and think of the details that are associated with this decision. We especially do not insist upon following a productive sequence in order to measure our degree of success. Instead we tend to address whatever situation appears to demand out skills and effort at the time. We rarely consider the impact upon our resources that these diversions cost us.

The discipline of learning how to prepare a grant proposal will also improve your prayer practices. Think of a grant proposal as a documented prayer with a purpose to serve God. You are making a request for support in order to be of service to others. Also because you do not want to waste the resources that God provides, you want to have a plan for carrying out the works that you propose.

The Holy Bible teaches that a man plans his ways but God orders his steps. The plans that we make need to be in line with what God wants us to do. The key is that we have to *believe* that we are doing God's will. We have to be in agreement that what we are doing is what God has purposed us to accomplish. The scriptures teach that all things are possible for those who believe.

The Difference Between Grant Writing and Proposal Writing

Technically speaking, there really is no difference between grant writing and proposal writing. The only difference in the two terms is found within the words themselves. Both grant writing and proposal writing offer the same outcome. Although someone writing a grant proposal may be hoping to obtain donations, the very same document could be used to obtain a bank loan for a startup business, etc., depending upon the project. This is one of the reasons that many non-profit organizations are able to obtain bridge loans from banks to cover overhead once they have received a grant award letter.

Today's standards for grant writing have been elevated to model the corporate standards for business proposal writing. For example, non-profit organizations that submit grant proposals generally have to include balance sheets, budgets and budget projections, project timelines, and even marketing plans to draw clients to their programs.

The term "grant writing" should actually be called "grant proposal writing." Grants are typically funds given based upon a proposed project, need or solution to a problem. People do not write grants. They write proposals to get the grants. Over the years, people have used the term "grant writing", perhaps without understanding that they would be required to write a proposal in order to receive a grant.

Grant proposal writing is often submitted as a response to a Request for Proposal, commonly referred to as RFP. An RFP is a document submitted by an entity with finances that is looking to pay for a solution, services, etc. The document states their guidelines and requirements for whoever would like to be awarded the money. Likewise, businesses looking for contractors may also issue an RFP.

As an instructor in both for-profit and non-profit development, I have helped people to establish their project plans so that they can be used in proposals for business as well as service development. Just as the contents of various business proposals may vary, so might the contents of various grant proposals. However, the basic structures and content of both grant writing and proposal writing are the same and may be used interchangeably.

There was a time when Foundations would only require minimal information in order to award grant dollars. However, grant making organizations such as the W. K. Kellogg Foundation, Bill Gates, The Ford Foundation and others have raised the bar for grant proposal writing. Even a growing number of smaller Foundations are requiring full blown proposals. In the past, many grantors only required short letters explaining the need for grant funding.

I still find it necessary to be mindful of what a client or student means and understands when they use the terms grant writing or proposal writing. I was once introduced as someone who writes grant proposals. The person responded, "You're just the person I need to talk to. Do you know any grant writers?"

What it Takes to Be a Good
Grant Proposal Writer

A good grant writer is someone who submits grant proposals that score high in the reviewing process. Grant writing is a form of communication that should compel the proposal reviewers to suggest your project for funding. A grant proposal needs to have high scores in order to get funded. In order to receive high scores, good grant writers should think more like grant reviewers and donors.

The grant writer should keep in mind that the first people to review their grant proposals are actually concerned with keeping their jobs. Their job is to examine your grant proposal and then determine if it should go beyond file 13 (AKA the trash can). Very rarely will your grants be scrutinized by the one writing the check. The check writer generally relies upon the summary of information and recommendations of the initial grant reviewer.

Studying the goals and objectives of a potential donor is another attribute of a good grant writer. The grant writer who is able to demonstrate that the project goals and objectives in the grant proposal line up with those of the donor, will have a better chance of getting past the initial review process.

The granting process is competitive, even though statistics show few grant proposals demonstrate the qualifications for the funds that they are requesting. Because of this competitive nature, a good grant proposal needs to have an element that says, " You will be very glad to have chosen me above the other grant proposals." A good grant writer must be competitive with the intention of writing what it takes to win the grant award.

A grant proposal is a detailed document that is submitted to propose a solution to a problem. The solution must illustrate a comprehensive plan, along with how much money and resources are needed to get the job done. The documents making the best case for being able to solve a problem are the ones that are "granted" the funding award. Therefore a good grant writer must be a strategic and detailed thinker.

In the world of grant making, the demands for evidence based solutions and accountability continue to grow. A good grant writer must stay abreast of the evolving standards for best practices and new innovations, in project delivery as well as evaluation processes.

Most importantly, a good grant writer must know how to follow instructions for submitting a grant proposal. The Freedom of Information Act allows people to request copies of government grant proposals that have been awarded. After reviewing a number of copies, I found that many of the grants awarded were not necessarily represented with quality writing skills. However, there was a consistency with supplying clear responses to the requested information. They generally followed the instructions to the letter.

Government grants offer the best training ground to become a good grant writer. This is because unlike what occurs with foundations, corporations and individual grants, grant writers receive details about why their grant proposals are denied or awarded funding. Once you receive high scores for a program grant from the federal government, you will know that you have what it takes to be a good grant writer.

Telling the Truth about Abilities

With so many people already finding it hard to believe in our abilities, I did not dare mention any of our technical skills in the grant proposal- which brings me to another lesson. It is essential to tell the truth about any technological enhancements, and let the reviewers sort it out. I only realized that this was the best way to do things after I became a grant reviewer.

If you have a technological ability that is little known, you may include it with a brief explanation about how and why it works with your project. Your challenge is convincing the reviewers that you truly understand what you state that you are using. It is not always necessary that *they* understand it as long as they are convinced that *you* understand it. You must also be able to show how this complicated technology will be effective with producing the results that you claim.

Grant proposal preparers would really benefit by first researching the acceptable standards for any activities that they plan to include. Even though your ideas are working and you are seeing results, if the rest of the world does not accept this as the norm, you need to go through a method of proving your experiences are valid.

Likewise, if the project is able to save time and money because of an innovation that you are using, you simply need to explain it. I did not explain what I stated because I had expected the reviewers to simply take my word that we could do it. This experience leads to another crucial lesson to learn. Since the reviewers do not know you, they have to be convinced that you are stating the truth and giving them facts. You have to somehow let them get to know and believe you.

Engaging Technology

In my grant proposals, the sections where I mentioned how our organization uses technology always gave me high scores. I would include our using Quickbooks Pro® to manage our financial activities and reporting. I would also describe how we used Microsoft® Access database to log our activities and other information.

However our technical abilities at the time that we submitted our first grant proposal actually did more harm than good. This was an area where I still disagree with the reviewers. There was a section where I was describing how long it would take for us to produce DVDs that featured drama addressing lifestyles and solutions regarding HIV/AIDS.

I had stated that it would take us 4-6 weeks to complete each DVD. The grant reviewers' comments stated that this was not a reasonable amount of time. In reality, it took us even less time than that because of the technology that we were using. Ours was a situation where the knowledgebase was not the same as what was generally known.

In our example, my husband and I had been challenged by the founder of H.O.P.E. International Outreach, Joseph Lemoine to produce a standalone DVD that would promote his organization's many accomplishments. We used a board member's video camera to get footage that we combined with some still photos.

We wanted to embed or place the video within the presentation that we developed in PowerPoint. At the time we were using Word Perfect Presentations, ULEAD along with Microsoft PowerPoint. Microsoft had a tool called Pack and Go that would allow people to view a presentation even if they did not have the full PowerPoint Package. Of the three packages, we preferred the cleanness with PowerPoint even though it was not the most versatile. When we tested the presentation on our system it always ran well. But when Mr. Lemoine tried to run it in his system he would only see a box and an x where the presentation was supposed to be. It did not take us more that 4 weeks total to develop a really good presentation. Of course we worked until we collapsed into the bed each night.

The proposal was based upon our experience and the formula for the format that we were using. However, as the grantee, we needed to convince the grantor that we had mastered a technology that they did not know existed.

Unfortunately, our proposal did not help the reviewers to understand that we had tapped into a little known ability at the time. Even the Microsoft support people did not know that their package could include an embedded video using their Pack and Go feature. I hounded the Microsoft support people by telephone and on-line to get them to tell me how to include video with myself running presentations on CD. They all told me the same thing. "You cannot have a self running CD with embedded video do it with this package." I stumbled upon how to do it by noticing that during the error process, the CD would be looking for the video from the file on the computer. So I simply copied all of the files onto a CD and reconstructed the presentation drawing the files from the CD instead of from the hard drive.

This may sound really technical, but it was only after praying along with my stubbornness did I realize that this could be done. Even though the experts stated that it could not be done, I had a gut feeling that it should be able to do this "one little thing" for the sake of our project. Anyway, it worked for us and Mr. Lemoine was quite pleased.

We went on to apply this new revelation to developing multimedia presentations that could be used for training and development. We got so good at it that we could actually complete the whole process in even less time. The only obstacle that would take us longer was that my husband was so picky about the sound. He would often go to his keyboards and develop the music scores for our scenes rather than use the canned sounds that I chose from the software package. He would cringe at most of the canned sounds and music that came with the software.

When it came to detailing our project in the grant proposal, I simply could not see that they would accept our little known ability to generate self running video-enhanced multi-media presentations using Microsoft PowerPoint. I did not see that it would benefit us to include that my husband is a gifted musician who scored our presentations with original music.

Many people already found it hard to believe that he could play and record audio tracks with all of the instrumentation, including drums (that actually sounded like real drums) along with strings, horns, etc. People often doubted our claim that our music and multi-media productions were generated in the petite studio that resided in our living room. We had to give people demonstrations to get them to see that it was even possible.

Demonstrate Your Use of Technology

Today's' computer arena offers a wide variety of solutions to enhance an organization's ability to function at maximum capacity. For example, documents are prepared on a word processor. Newsletters are prepared using a Desktop publishing application.

My experience has shown that an obstacle that prevents grass roots organizations from harnessing the efficiency of technology and office automation is the "digital divide." Many grass roots organizations simply lack the time and resources to gain the appropriate knowledge that would help them to develop a workable technology strategy.

If an organization has a firm grasp of the basics, then they can take advantage of the services of a consultant that would help them to design the most cost effective and efficient solutions. For example, if an organization does not have access to a computer system and a word processor, that organization will not produce documents and letters as efficiently as other organizations that do have that capability. When or if organizations find the need to upgrade to a more efficient application or system, they need to first understand the capabilities of what they already have.

Nonprofit organizations should conduct self assessments to help determine their technology needs. Each organization must be assessed according to their organizational makeup as well as their goals and objectives. Effective technology assessments will take into account the present status along with future projections.

TechAtlas is an online tool that provides a free technology assessment tool. It is a very useful on-line tool that provides: Articles, Resources, and Worksheets, to help you learn more about what technical terms mean, such as RAM, Operating Systems, and Hard Drives, networks and more. The TechAtlas Planning Center and TechSurveyor Asset Management Center both include a glossary of Technology Terms, nonprofit-friendly explanations of technology concepts, and links to resources to learn more.

Sometimes, you can even use a worksheet to take your new information and make it work for your organization. Example resource topics include: Staffing for Technology, Budgeting for On-Going Technology Costs and Fundraising for New Technology.

The internet is a widely used database that provides connectivity and access to a vast universe of services, products and information. Organizations that have internet capabilities will be able to develop at a much better pace than those who do not have internet access. The options provided through the internet can greatly enhance the process of planning for technological enhancements.

Technology planning is being practiced by nonprofit organizations so that they can become more productive and sustaining. According to an on-line technology assistance organization called TechSoup, "a technology plan is the single most important ingredient to effectively using technology in your organization. The technology planning process will help minimize technology-related crises, use staff time efficiently, and avoid wasting money on equipment. Create a plan to help you think through your priorities in order to use technology in a way that directly furthers your mission."

TechSoup is one of the nation's oldest and largest nonprofit technology assistance agencies. Their services are open to all qualified 501c3 nonprofit organizations. The TechSoup website is powered by CompuMentor. TechSoup.org offers nonprofits a one-stop resource for technology needs by providing free information, resources, and support. In addition to online information and resources, they offer a product philanthropy service called TechSoup Stock. Nonprofits can access donated and discounted technology products.

TechSoup provides instructional articles and worksheets for nonprofit staff members who utilize information technologies, as well as technology planning information for executives and other decision makers. Their introductory articles and message board support are aimed at those who do not have much experience using technology; however they also provide more advanced information.

Another advantage with today's technology is the ability to connect with masses of people easily and inexpensively. I was able to connect with over 5,000 people in less than 30 days just by writing articles that were published online. I even got paid for writing.

A Reason why Your Tax Exempt Status is Not Enough to Get a Grant

As a grant reviewer, I learned that many times having a 501 (c) (3) tax exempt status is not enough to receive certain grant dollars. The tax exempt status simply means that you are able to conduct business as a non-profit entity. There is no limit with regards to the number of staff you must hire. You also have a great deal of flexibility with deciding upon the services that you want to provide.

But what uninformed organizations do not know is that many of them are being turned down for grants because of the size of their budgets. The reasoning is that since you have not handled large sums of money already, you cannot be trusted to effectively manage a sizable grant award.

We were able to receive large amounts of grant dollars because we came under the umbrella of a management organization that specializes in helping organizations to get their foot in the door. Organizations like this can help start ups to focus on their service development without having to be concerned with the fiscal management of their program.

A good management organization will handle the incoming funds as well as keep track of all transactions and related reporting. Our even files the 990 tax form on our behalf. Their books are the ones that get audited on behalf of our program. I just have to address my own personal tax concerns.

Using a management organization as an umbrella worked so well for me that I learned how to do this for others. In fact, I helped a brand new (two years young) organization to receive over $300,000 dollars in federal grant dollars without having their own tax exempt status. This is significant because there is a special government audit that organizations experience if they receive over $300,000. The government requires that you contract an independent auditor to account for your expenditures. Our organization has always passed our audits with flying colors.

It is encouraging to meet well meaning individuals who want to do something to make a difference in the world. I encounter large numbers of people who express an interest in starting a non-profit organization in order to get tax exempt donations. However the high cost of filing fee (now $750) seems a bit much for start ups.

Many are also discouraged by the intimidating form that must accompany the fee. However, there is a way to get your foot in the door without going through this process.

You can form your start up project and use a fiscal agent to receive donations.

How to Get Non-profit Donations without Having Your Own 501 (c) (3) Tax Exempt Status

There are some basic steps that you should take in order to prepare to get a fiscal agent or engage an adoption organization offering monitoring and more involved support.

- Decide that you are going to specialize in a particular area of need such as homelessness, illiteracy, etc.
- Determine what type of people you will be serving, which is called your target population. For example you may decide to serve at risk homeless youth between the ages of 7 and 13.

- Identify the primary target location that you will be serving. It is generally best to serve an area with which you know has a great need. This area may be an urban community or rural. But be specific about the geographic location using descriptions such as (for example) *"the inner city community of Lawndale in Chicago, Illinois."*

- Decide what service you are going to offer, how you will carry it out and how much it will cost per person to provide the service.

- Find a location where your service(s) can be provided. You may provide this service at a location that is already established such as a school, library, community center, church, etc. Make sure that you get a written agreement that you may use this facility for a set period of time.

- Neatly document the detailed plans for your project so that you and others will know what you are doing.

- Contact an organization to ask them to serve as your fiscal agent to offer you the tax exempt status needed for receiving donations. (See the Resource below for a national option). Any organization with a 501 (c)(3) tax exempt status in good standing may serve as your fiscal agent. The fiscal agent will also be responsible for completing the tax reporting to reflect what you received and paid. You will only be responsible for reporting your personal income received as wages. Donors simply need a means of writing off their donations in order to have tax breaks.

A fiscal agent will generally charge anywhere from 3.85% to 10% of your income in order to manage (receive and disburse) your funds.

Make sure that the fiscal agent that you choose files 990 tax returns. Ask to see a copy of the most recent return. If the organization has not received the amount of money that you are planning to get, find another organization.

We use Congressional District Programs as a management organization because they go far beyond the services of a fiscal agent. The website is www.cdprograms.org. You can get a discounted sign up fee if you let them know that you learned about them from Dr. Margaret Jamal's book.

"Planting Good Works to Produce Good Fruit"

Appendices

Resources

Web site
www.faithlegacies.org

blog
www.faithlegacies.blogspot.com

Other Titles by Dr. Margaret Jamal

My Grant Writing Secrets

National Treasures-U.S. Foundation Grants

R.A.T.E.S. Principles
for
Organizational Development

When Girls Don't Tell

Determine the Problem Table

Place an X in the box(es) next to the problem where the statement is true.

Problems (List the problems that you have experienced)	I strongly desire to eliminate this problem	This problem has caused me personal pain & suffering	I am personally responsible for doing something about this problem	It disturbs me to hear about someone else suffering from this problem	God has called me to help eliminate this problem	TOTALS
1.						
2.						
3.						
4.						
5.						

Focus on the Problem Worksheet

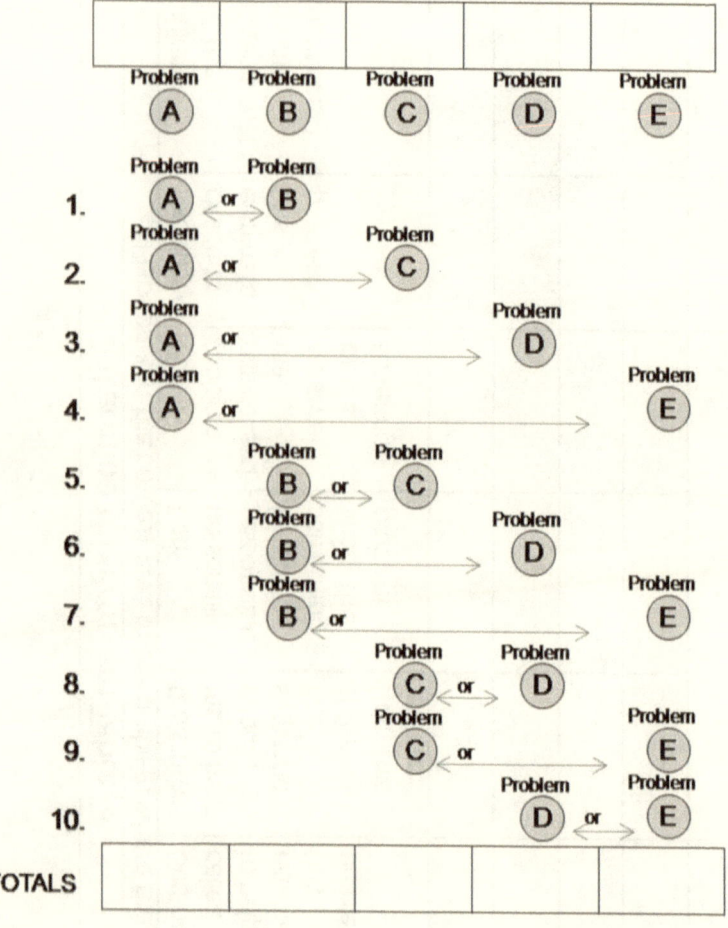

	Problem A	Problem B	Problem C	Problem D	Problem E
1.	A	or B			
2.	A	or	C		
3.	A	or		D	
4.	A	or			E
5.		B	or C		
6.		B	or	D	
7.		B	or		E
8.			C	or D	
9.			C	or	E
10.				D	or E
TOTALS					

Instructions for the Activity Planning Table (*part 1*)

1.   Activity-Describe the task that needs to be completed. (Ex. Objective: recruit 50 clients; Activity: Prepare artwork for 10,000 flyers.

2.   Recipient- Describe who is receiving the service or who will directly benefit from completion of this task (Ex. Unemployed Hispanic Teens age 16-18)

3.   Responsible Party-Give the job title for the one who is accountable for completing this task. (Ex. Administrative Assistant)

4.   Day(s)/Time(s) -Begin and complete the task. (Ex. Tuesdays & Thursdays 8:30-11:00 for 2 weeks)

5.   Month/ Quarter -Indicate the month and quarter for this task to be completed. (Ex. Jan; 1st Qtr)

6.   Support Personnel/Consultants -List the type of help and titles of the people that will be needed in order to complete this task. (Ex. For the task to complete a promotional flyer this project may use a Graphic Designer for flyer artwork and a Project Director for oversight and artwork content and an Administrative Assistant for correspondence and general administration. The Project Director would be the responsible party and the Graphic Designer would be a support personnel or consultant along with the Administrative Assistant.

7.   Equipment/Facilities Needed-List all of the equipment as well as space that will be utilized in order to complete this task. (Ex. Computer for correspondence, Copy machine, Fax machine, 2,000 square feet of Office space)

Activities and Resources Planning Table

1-Activity #	2-Recipient (client, staff)	3-Responsible Party	4-Days/ Time Beginning- Ending	5-Month/ Quarter
6-Support Personnel/Consultants	7-Equipment/Space Needed	8-Supplies Needed	9- Consultant/P ersonnel Fees	10- Equipment Supplies Cost/Fees
				11-TOTAL COST

Instructions for the Activity Planning Table (*part 2*)

8.   Supplies Needed-List all of the supplies that will be consumed or used in order to complete this task. (Ex. Copy paper, Ink, Envelopes, Stamps)

9.   Consultant/ Personnel Fees-Estimate the cost for each staff member needed to complete this task. (Ex. Graphic Designer $350, Project Director $450, Admin $250)

10.   Equipment/Supplies fees, lease, etc.-Estimate the cost for the equipment, facilities rental/leases and supplies that will be used for this task. (Ex. $200-computer equipment, $150 space rental, $75 supplies)

11.   Total Cost- Indicate the total cost for personnel and other items that will be needed to complete the task given (Ex. $1,475)

Activities and Resources Planning Table

1-Activity #	2-Recipient (client, staff)	3-Responsible Party	4-Days/ Time Beginning- Ending	5-Month/ Quarter
6-Support Personnel/Consultants	7-Equipment/Space Needed	8-Supplies Needed	9- Consultant/P ersonnel Fees	10- Equipment Supplies Cost/Fees
			11-TOTAL COST	

INDEX OF SUB TOPICS

INDEX OF KEY WORDS

www.ingramcontent.com/pod-product-compliance
Lightning Source LLC
Chambersburg PA
CBHW021818170526
45157CB00007B/2639